THE
BUCCANEERS

This book is dedicated to all Buccaneer air and ground crews,
in remembrance of our colleagues who failed to return,
in particular my close friend,
Squadron Leader 'Jock' Gilroy,
killed on 4 January 1972.

THE BUCCANEERS

OPERATIONAL SERVICE WITH THE ROYAL NAVY AND ROYAL AIR FORCE

Air Commodore Graham Pitchfork MBE, BA, FRAeS

Foreword by
Air Chief Marshal Sir Michael Knight

Patrick Stephens Limited
AN IMPRINT OF HAYNES PUBLISHING

First published in 2002

British Library Cataloguing in Publication Data
A catalogue record for this book is available from the British Library

ISBN 1-85260-611-8

Patrick Stephens Limited is an imprint of
Haynes Publishing, Sparkford,
Nr Yeovil, Somerset, BA22 7JJ.

Typeset in 10/14 pt Sabon.
Typesetting and origination by
Sutton Publishing Limited.
Printed and bound in England by
J.H. Haynes & Co. Ltd, Sparkford.

Contents

Acknowledgements

I would like to express my thanks to all who have given help in the preparation of this book and particularly those who have provided contributions and parted, temporarily, with precious photographs and notes. The number is large but my first thanks are to my old 'Boss', Air Chief Marshal Sir Mike Knight. As a Buccaneer pilot and President of the Buccaneer Aircrew Association, no one is better qualified to introduce this book and I am very grateful to him for his eloquent and generous words. I would also like to thank him for his wise counsel, expert advice and support.

The Director of the Air Historical Branch and his excellent staff have given me much help and I am particularly grateful to Tony Stevens, Steve Clarke and Brian Maidment. Gerry Shores and his staff at the Fleet Air Arm Museum have been very helpful and I also want to thank Peter March, the Editor of the RAF Yearbook, for his help and advice. Very many of my Buccaneer colleagues have assisted me and I would like to single out Tom Eeles, Dave Herriot and Rick Phillips for their contributions and a great deal of advice, not least answering countless telephone calls and e-mails and reading the drafts. I hope my other colleagues will not be offended if I list them in alphabetical order. Ken Alley, Vice-Admiral Sir Ted Anson, Air Marshal Sir Peter Bairsto, Al Beaton, Nick Berryman, Vic Blackwood, Tom Bradley, Norman Browne, Mike Bush, Malcolm Caygill, Bruce Chapple, Barry Chown, Dave Cleland-Smith, Tim Cockerell, Bill Cope, Frank Cox, Dr Mike Edwards, Air Commodore Pete Eustace, Andy Evans, Air Commodore Jon Ford, John Fraser, 'Hoddy' Hoddinott, 'Dutch' Holland, David Howard, Air Commodore Ben Laite, Captain 'Spiv' Leahy RN, Tony Lunnon-Wood, Mike Maddox, Bob McLellan, 'Pony' Moore, Hilton Moses, Dave Mulinder, John Myers, Air Vice-Marshal Bob O'Brien, Tony Ogilvy, Philip Pinney, Bob Poots, John Plumb, Dave Ray, Bill Ryce, Mike Scarffe, Air Commodore Graham Smart, Gary Stapleton, Peter Sturt, Captain David Thompson RN, Ron Trinder, Peter Walwyn, Niall Watson, Mick Whybro, Air Commodore Dave Wilby, Air Commodore Phil Wilkinson, Rear Admiral Sir Robert Woodard, Air Vice-Marshal Rob Wright, Eddie Wyer. I thank all of them most sincerely.

On the photograph front I want to thank the Controller of The Stationery Office for permission to use MOD Crown Copyright photographs. I also thank Paul Lawson of the BAe Systems Heritage Centre at Brough for obtaining permission to use BAe photographs and Mary Hudson at the Air Historical Branch who has been most helpful. I am also grateful to Robert Rudhall at *Flypast* magazine. Many colleagues have provided photographs and I hope they will accept the acknowledgement accompanying the photographs as a token of my thanks for their help.

Finally, I want to thank Jonathan Falconer, Elizabeth Stone and the staff at Sutton Publishing for all their help and advice.

Foreword

Air Chief Marshal Sir Michael Knight KCB AFC FRAeS President, The Buccaneer Aircrew Association

There have been a number of books already published on the history of that great British combat aircraft, the British Aerospace (Blackburn) Buccaneer. To my knowledge, none has treated the in-service, operational aspects of the story with anything approaching the detail – let alone the conviction – that Graham Pitchfork has brought to it.

In truth, there can be few better qualified for the task. To his vast experience as a front-line Buccaneer observer and navigator with both the Fleet Air Arm and the Royal Air Force, can be added his highly successful tours as instructor, Flight and Squadron Commander and the credibility which all of that brought to successive 'front-line' staff appointments. And if that were not enough, his facility with the pen and his deeply ingrained love of military – particularly aviation – history are merely the icing on a splendidly rich cake.

In researching this invaluable addition to the library of aerospace literature, Graham has obviously drawn heavily on his own aforementioned experience. But, typical of the man, he has done more. The many, very relevant, quotations from fellow-Buccaneer operators and their ever-faithful ground crew supporters, both dark and light blue, add greatly to the sense of immediacy and to the absolute authority which make this a compelling read. And that must surely hold good not only for those favoured by membership of the Buccaneer fraternity but, if they can bear it, for the aircrews of those very many less distinguished types of military aircraft.

From the earliest days of the Royal Navy's Buccaneer Mark (ex-NA 39) to the last exciting months of the S2B in RAF service, this is a comprehensive and thoroughly readable work. As with any serious volume of aviation history, there are a few sad (and rather more 'hairy') episodes to relate. That said, the book is certainly not lacking the occasional touch of humour and, in particular, the overarching sense of *bonhomie* that were – and are – the hallmarks of the Buccaneer force.

For understandable reasons, the story of that famous aircraft in service with the South African Air Force has not been told in this book. One may only hope that it might inspire one or more of our colleagues from that gallant band to take up the challenge. For it is, after all, only in South African skies that the magnificent old lady may still be seen – and heard. And what a loss that is for those hundreds of thousands who faithfully and regularly flock to the British air display circuit. Like that genuine TSR2 replacement, the ill-fated 'Buccaneer 2-star', here was yet another lost opportunity for the nation; but is that not the story of all our lives? At least some of us can look back with pride and delight to those glorious Buccaneering days of yore.

Abbreviations

A&AEE	Aircraft & Armament Experimental Establishment
AAA	Anti-Aircraft Artillery
AAR	Air-to-Air Refuelling
ADD	Airflow Direction Detector
ADSL	Auto Depressed Sight Line
AFNORTH	Allied Forces Northern Europe
AI	Air Intercept
AOC	Air Officer Commanding
APC	Armament Practice Camp
AR	Anti-Radiation
ASM	Airfield Survival Measures
AWI	Air Warfare Instructor
BAI	Battlefield Air Interdiction
BAI	Buccaneer Attack Instructor
BALTAP	Baltic Approaches
BBC	British Broadcasting Corporation
BLC	Boundary Layer Control
CAP	Combat Air Patrol
CBLS	Carrier Bomb Light Store
CBU	Cluster Bomb Unit
CCA	Carrier Controlled Approach
CFS	Central Flying School
CO	Commanding Officer
COC	Combined Operations Centre
COMTWOATAF	Commander Second Allied Tactical Air Force
CRISP	Continuous Radar Intelligence Surface Plot
CTTO	Central Trials & Tactics Organisation
DFC	Designated Flying Course
DH	Direct Hit
DLP	Deck Landing Practice
ECM	Electronic Counter Measure
ETPS	Empire Test Pilots' School
EW	Electronic Warfare
EWI	Electronic Warfare Instructor
FAC	Forward Air Controller
FDO	Flight Deck Officer
Flyco	Flying Control
FOB	Forward Operating Base
FPB	Fast Patrol Boat
GCI	Ground Control Intercept
GDP	Gun Direction Platform
HAS	Hardened Aircraft Shelter
HE	High Explosive
HES	High Explosive Substitute
HMS	Her Majesty's Ship
HUD	Head-up Display
IFIS	Integrated Flight Instrumentation System
IGV	Inlet Guide Vane
IN	Inertial Navigation
IP	Initial Point
JMC	Joint Maritime Course
LGB	Laser-Guided Bomb
LOPRO	Low Probe
LSO	Landing Sight Officer
MADDLs	Mirror-Assisted Dummy Deck Landing
Martel	Missile Anti-Radiation Television
MPA	Maritime Patrol Aircraft
NATO	North Atlantic Treaty Organisation
OCA	Offensive Counter Air

OCU	Operational Conversion Unit
ORI	Operational Readiness Inspection
PAI	Pilot Attack Instructor
PB	Practice Bomb
PBF	Pilots' Briefing Facility
QFI	Qualified Flying Instructor
QRA	Quick Reaction Alert
QWI	Qualified Weapons Instructor
RAE	Royal Aircraft Establishment
RAF	Royal Air Force
RDAF	Royal Danish Air Force
RNAS	Royal Naval Air Station
RN	Royal Navy
RNethAF	Royal Netherlands Air Force
RNoAF	Royal Norwegian Air Force
RPM	Revolutions Per Minute
RSO	Range Safety Officer
RWR	Radar Warning Receiver
SACEUR	Supreme Allied Commander Europe
SACLANT	Supreme Allied Commander Atlantic
SAG	Surface Action Group
SAM	Surface-to-Air Missile
SAP	Simulated Attack Profile
SAR	Search and Rescue
SARBE	Search and Rescue Beacon Equipment
SOP	Standard Operating Procedure
SURPIC	Surface Picture
TACDI	Tactical Direction
Taceval	Tactical Evaluation
TASMO	Tactical Air Support of Maritime Operations
TVAT	TV Airborne Trainer
UKADR	United Kingdom Air Defence Region
USAF	United States Air Force
USN	United States Navy
VT	Variable Timed

Introduction

This book concentrates on the flying activities of the Buccaneer squadrons and the men who flew and serviced the aircraft in Royal Navy and Royal Air Force service. It is not intended to be the definitive history of the aircraft and, thus, the technical content is limited to providing an adequate background to the main theme. Those who want to learn more about the design, development and early trials work of the Buccaneer are strongly recommended to consult Roy Boot's excellent book, *From Spitfire to Eurofighter* published by Airlife.

Military ranks and decorations referred to in the narrative are those held at the time of the activity described. They are not repeated for additional quotes except where the rank had changed.

The limited size of this book, and the use of so many photographs, has meant that many activities could not be covered. Very reluctantly, no mention is made of the sterling service the aircraft gave in the South African Air Force. Also, there was insufficient space to mention the crucially important trials work carried out by the aircraft and its crews in support of the front-line squadrons. The aircraft was in operational service for over thirty years, and there are very many events and activities that cannot be covered in the space available. This in no way is meant to suggest that they are unimportant, but I have tried to present a wide cross-section to illustrate the diversity of Buccaneer activities and operating techniques. In this way, I hope I have captured the main features of this outstanding aircraft – and the unique atmosphere and sense of comradeship that was all-pervasive in the Buccaneer fraternity.

Graham Pitchfork

CHAPTER 1

Background and Development

In November 1940, twenty-one elderly Swordfish biplanes took off from HMS *Illustrious* and effectively destroyed the Italian Fleet at Taranto. Just six months later, in May 1941, the torpedo-carrying Swordfish of HMS *Ark Royal* crippled the *Bismarck* and sealed the fate of the mighty German battleship. Within a few months, carrier-borne aircraft of the Imperial Japanese Navy had wreaked havoc at Pearl Harbor and, three days later, sent two of the Royal Navy's battleships, HMS *Prince of Wales* and HMS *Repulse*, to the bottom of the South China Sea. As the war came to an end in 1945, aircraft-carriers operating in the Pacific had formed the cornerstone of the Allied victory against the Japanese. The reach and devastating power provided by carrier-borne aircraft had been amply demonstrated and the aircraft-carrier had quite clearly replaced the battleship as the capital ships of the Fleet.

The end of the Second World War may have seen the demise of the menace of Nazism and Japanese Imperialism but it would soon herald an uneasy peace, and the outbreak of the Korean War in 1950 emphasised the dangers inherent in the new world order of the 'Cold War'. The Soviet Navy had previously been limited to coastal operations geared to the defence of the Soviet Union, but a significant increase in the warship-building programme highlighted the emergence of a global capability posing a great threat to the security of the vital sea-borne trade of the Western Powers. Pre-eminent in the Soviet shipbuilding programme was the development of the 17,000-ton, heavily gun-armed *Sverdlov* cruiser.

During the war years there had been major developments in radar technology and the capability to detect high-flying aircraft at long range had been achieved. However, the shape of the earth dictated that an aircraft flying just above the surface would not enter the 'lobe' of enemy radar until it reached a range of some twenty-six miles. Flying at high speed and low level, an attacking aircraft would give a target as little as three minutes' warning of an impending attack. The surprise element of such an attack had been recognised by the staff of the Naval Air Warfare Division, and in 1952 they realised that this was the answer to the threat posed by the *Sverdlov*. The following year the Navy Board issued Specification M.148T for a two-seat, carrier-based strike aircraft capable of delivering nuclear and conventional weapons over long ranges and at high speed. This culminated in the issue of Naval Air Requirement NA 39 the following year.

The Requirement specified that the primary role of the aircraft was to be the attack of ships at sea or large coastal targets, which would be radar-discreet and identifiable at long range. The primary weapons were listed as the 'Green

A Soviet Navy *Sverdlov* cruiser. The Buccaneer was designed to a specific Royal Navy requirement to counter the heavily gun-armed cruiser. This photograph was taken from a Buccaneer on 26 March 1971, when the cruiser was refuelling in the South-West Approaches. (*Author*)

Cheese' anti-ship homing bomb and a tactical nuclear bomb, with an additional requirement to deliver a large range of secondary weapons. The aircraft was also to be capable of acting as an air-to-air refuelling tanker. The operational profile envisaged a 400-mile radius of action, with a descent from high level to very low level just outside the detection range of a target's radar, followed by a high-speed low-level dash to and from the target. Stringent weight limits were imposed and the aircraft had to be capable of operating and being supported from the Royal Navy's current aircraft-carriers. This imposed maximum take-off and landing weights and the aircraft size had to allow it to be lowered to the ship's hangar by the lifts.

The naval requirement set a daunting technical challenge, but most of the major British aircraft companies submitted designs. At the end of March 1954 five companies were invited to tender for the order of twenty development aircraft. The Blackburn and General Aircraft Company at Brough were successful with their B 103 design and the initial go-ahead for production was given in July 1955. Although a small company compared to other British aircraft manufacturers, Blackburns had a long history of producing aircraft for the Royal Navy; but B 103 was their first venture into the jet age. Dr Mike Edwards was a key member of the Blackburn development team and he summarised the requirement as:

> A remarkably far-sighted specification involving low level, under the radar lobe attacks at long range and high sub-sonic speeds, characteristics that endured for almost fifty years. All the more remarkable as this happened less than ten years after their Lordships were operating the Swordfish in front-line service.

Achieving the necessary landing speeds for carrier operations posed a particularly difficult challenge and most companies utilised the benefits of 'jet deflection', which was at the early stages of development. Blackburns investigated the benefit of boundary-layer control, achieved by blowing high-pressure air, bled from the engines, over the leading edges of the wing and tailplane and over the flaps and ailerons in order to obtain increased lift and thus reduce landing speed. The net value of these measures was an approach speed with full flap and aileron droop some seventeen knots slower than an 'unblown' approach. This method provided significant advantages over the 'jet deflection' method and also allowed the Blackburn design to employ a smaller wing – an important feature for high-speed low-level flight. The need to generate high bleed-air pressure from the engines for the approach and landing phase resulted in a high engine rpm and an unacceptable landing speed. A large airbrake, forming part of the aft fuselage, was the answer – fully extended, the appropriate approach speed could be maintained and this became the standard landing configuration for the aircraft. A T-tail had already been selected, the position of the airbrake having made this inevitable.

Another advanced feature was the embodiment of an 'area rule' design, which allowed a reduction in the amount of thrust required to maintain maximum cruising speed. This offered the bonus of a larger internal rear fuselage size for the storage of avionics and fuel. The structure of the aircraft was based on two large machined steel spars used in the inner wing, with integrally stiffened machined skins on the thin wings and the all-moving tailplane giving the aircraft added strength. Generations of Buccaneer aircrew have extolled the virtue of their aircraft's strength over the years. To some it was akin to the proverbial brick-built s***house! The folding nose contained the radar, and the design of a 180° rotating bomb door for an internal bomb bay capable of carrying 4,000 lb of stores was unusual and would provide an added bonus in later years when an external fuel tank was incorporated in the skin of the bomb door.

Selection of the engines presented some difficulties and, eventually, a scaled-down de Havilland Gyron producing just over 7,000 lb of thrust was selected. Two engines gave the desired sea-level cruising speed of Mach 0.85 and just sufficient thrust for take-off. It is interesting to note the comments made by an independent audit carried out by American officials who made the telling remarks, 'the airplane seems underpowered and pitch-up could be a problem'. Time would prove them right.

Just thirty-three months after Blackburns had been given the go-ahead, the first aircraft (XK 486) was ready for taxi trials. Mike Edwards justifiably makes the comment:

> For such a relatively small design and production team, on what for its day was a very advanced project, this represented a remarkable achievement, and particularly when compared with the ponderous progress we see on some projects today.

By March 1958, the aircraft was ready for engine runs, and these were completed at the company airfield at Brough, near Hull. The small airfield was totally unsuited to operate the NA 39 and the company arranged to lease the former bomber airfield at Holme-on-Spalding-Moor, some 18 miles from the factory. However, the Ministry of Supply deemed that the 6,000-ft runway at Holme was still too short for the first flight, so XK 486 was partially dismantled, covered in a shroud and transported by road to the Royal Aircraft Establishment's airfield at Bedford. Blackburn's recently appointed Chief Test Pilot, Derek Whitehead, an experienced former Royal Navy test pilot, commenced taxi trials in April. These trials suffered an early setback when a tyre blew out and damaged the starboard inner wing skin, but the engineers soon had the aircraft ready for

The first NA 39 was transported to Bedford on a trailer, shrouded from the gaze of onlookers. Traditional traffic makes way for the nuclear bomber. (*BAe Systems*)

its first flight, which took place on 30 April with Whitehead at the controls and the Head of Flight Testing, Bernard Watson, in the rear seat. The first flight was made without using the boundary-layer control system and the 39-minute flight was a complete success. After a further three months of testing at Bedford the aircraft finally returned to Holme and the test programme continued. Further aircraft became available and they were towed along local roads, in the early hours of the morning, from the factory at Brough to Holme airfield where they made their first flights before being allocated to specific tasks for the flight test programme.

More pilots were converted to the NA 39 before joining the flight test team. One of these, Lieutenant-Commander Ted Anson, an experienced Royal Navy test pilot, recalls his introduction to the new aircraft:

> Although I had just completed a tour in an embarked Scimitar squadron, I was told by a Ministry official that it was necessary to fly four sorties in a Hunter from the 6,000-ft runway at Holme, followed by four more sorties in a Meteor NF 14 for twin-engine practice! Only then could I go to Boscombe Down for a first familiarisation sortie in the NA 39. It was mandatory, he said, that the first five training sorties should be flown from a runway at least 9,000 ft long. All this logic defied me. My conversion programme coincided with Farnborough week and the display aircraft had gone unserviceable and I was asked to fly another aircraft from Boscombe to Holme for it to be prepared for the display. So my fourth familiarisation flight was a trip from Boscombe to land on the 6,000-ft runway at Holme. Strange how the rules change when it is convenient!

Ted Anson went on to become 'Mr Buccaneer Royal Navy,' filling every Buccaneer appointment up to Captain of HMS *Ark Royal* before retiring as a Vice-Admiral.

The NA 39 made its public debut at the SBAC Show at Farnborough in September 1959, when Derek Whitehead and 'Sailor' Parker demonstrated XK 490. Shortly afterwards this aircraft was lost, with its crew, when it crashed in the New Forest, and the carrier deck trials scheduled for later in the month had to be delayed until the investigation was completed into the cause of this tragic accident. The deck

With the hook down, Derek Whitehead brings XK 523 over the round-down of HMS *Victorious* for the first deck landing on 19 January 1960. The ship is steaming in Lyme Bay at 25 kts, into the wind, giving a wind over the deck of some 40 kts. (*BAe Systems*)

trials finally took place on board HMS *Victorious* in the following January, and Derek Whitehead, flying XK 523, made the first carrier landing on 19 January 1960 in difficult weather conditions. A second aircraft, XK 489, the first 'navalised' aircraft, joined the programme and thirty-one successful sorties were completed, together with important deck handling, aircraft lift and hangar stowage trials.

As more of the development-batch aircraft became available the flight test programme gathered momentum. Lessons learned from earlier trials were embodied in the newer aircraft and minor structural changes were made. Hot-weather trials were conducted in Malta, weapon trials commenced at West Freugh, and three aircraft were attached to A&AEE Boscombe Down for completion of the Controller Aircraft (CA) Release, obtained in April 1961. These trials by 'C' Squadron at Boscombe included full carrier trials, some being conducted from HMS *Ark Royal* in the Mediterranean during January 1961. One aircraft (XK 526) was then shipped to Singapore for tropical trials. In the meantime, the aircraft had finally been given a name and, on 26 August 1960, the NA 39 acquired the very appropriate designation of Buccaneer S 1, the 'S' indicating the aircraft's strike (nuclear) capability.

One trial that encountered major problems, resulting in a complete re-design, was the air-to-

With the undercarriage and hook down, XK 489 makes a slow pass over the runway during the September 1960 Farnborough Air Show. (*P.H.T. Green*)

air refuelling trial conducted behind Valiant tankers. Mike Edwards explains:

> The first retractable air-to-air refuelling probe was a model of neatness; unfortunately it did not work. The aerodynamic bow wave over the nose of the aircraft carried the tanker's refuelling drogue up and away before the probe could engage, to the intense frustration of the pilots. When extended, the probe was almost directly in line with the engine intake and engine banging occurred. A modification was designed and guaranteed to work, but to everyone's dismay, the flight tests showed little improvement. On one occasion a frustrated pilot managed to hit the rim of the drogue but only succeeded in breaking off the probe, which flew down the starboard engine intake with predictable results on engine health. The answer – a large fixed probe – and there were no further problems.

As the manufacturer's and Boscombe Down trials continued, the Royal Navy formed its first unit with the specific task of developing operational and engineering techniques and capabilities.

CHAPTER 2

Early Fleet Air Arm Operations

The Royal Navy's Buccaneer Intensive Flying Trials Unit, 700Z Flight, was formed at RNAS Lossiemouth (HMS *Fulmar*) on 7 March 1961, when Rear Admiral F.H.E. Hopkins CB DSO DSC, the Flag Officer Naval Flying Training, took the salute at the commissioning parade held in Hangar Two. Lieutenant-Commander Alan 'Spiv' Leahy DSC, a highly experienced ground-attack pilot and Korean War veteran, commanded the flight. Since the flight had formed before delivery of the first Buccaneer aircraft, Derek Whitehead flew one to Lossiemouth to provide an appropriate backdrop for the parade.

The Flight formed with twenty-four officers and 124 maintenance ratings and was equipped with two-seat Hunters, Meteors and a Seahawk, which allowed the pilots to remain in current flying practice. Most had experience on Seahawk and Scimitars and the observers were drawn from the Sea Vixen, Gannet and Wessex squadrons. Before the first Buccaneer arrived, the air and

The aircrew and engineer officers of 700Z Flight pose in front of the unit's first aircraft, XK 531, at Lossiemouth in August 1961. The Commanding Officer, Commander 'Spiv' Leahy, is in the centre of the back row with Lieutenant-Commander Ted Anson on his right. (*BAe Systems*)

ground crews travelled to Brough and Edinburgh where they learned about the aircraft, weapon systems and engines. In July the Commanding Officer and Lieutenants 'Hoddy' Hoddinott and Brian Toomey left for Boscombe Down where they were converted to the Buccaneer. The following month the first two Buccaneers (XK 531 and XK 532) were flown to Lossiemouth by Bobby Burns, a Blackburn test pilot, and Brian Toomey, and the eager ground crew immediately started the acceptance checks. Ted Anson arrived as Senior Pilot and the conversion programme for the remainder of the pilots was started. One of the first to complete the conversion was Lieutenant Bill Ryce, who recalls:

> I joined 700Z Flight when it formed in early 1961 but patience was required as we had no aircraft and it was August before I actually flew the Buccaneer S 1. In the meantime I flew all sorts of other aircraft – Hunter T8 & GA11, Sea Hawk, Vampire T22, Sea Devon, Sea Prince, and two biplanes, the Dominie and Tiger Moth. What a great life!
>
> When I finally got airborne in the Buccaneer it was with the redoubtable John Coleman, our Senior Observer, in the back seat. At once I felt at home and immediately appreciated the aircraft's potential for low-level work. Until this time I had only flown single-seat, front-line aircraft and I soon came to appreciate the luxury of flying with another crew member. There was always someone to share one's problems with, and the Buccaneer S1 did present us with the odd problem! However, I view my early Buccaneer days as a highlight in my flying career.

As more aircraft arrived the trials programme was expanded and, by October, twenty-five sorties were being flown each week. These included fuel consumption checks at various heights, radio altimeter trials and general handling. The Senior Observer, Lieutenant-Commander John Coleman, monitored navigation trials and weapon systems and the Blue Parrot radar once it arrived, replacing the lump of lead in the nose. The flight reached full complement of six aircraft in December 1961 with the delivery of the last two, which appeared in the overall white 'anti-flash' scheme similar to that adopted by the RAF's V-bomber fleet. The availability of these new aircraft allowed over 100 hours to be flown each month. Further progress was made by the positioning of a radar reflector target at the nearby weapons range at Tain for trials with the weapon system and the assessment of dummy bombing profiles. Unfortunately, the

One of the first aircraft to join 700Z Flight was XK 534, seen here with the Lossiemouth fin code 'LM'. (*MAP*)

Controller of Aircraft release to drop weapons was not issued during the existence of the flight, but sorties were flown with the bomb bay loaded with four inert 1,000-lb bombs, giving the crews experience of handling the aircraft at high all-up weights. By the middle of the year the formation of the first operational squadron was imminent and the flight was given the additional task of training the new air and ground crews. Some of the most experienced members of the Flight were transferred to form the nucleus of the new 801 Squadron.

Many other tasks fell to the flight including demonstration flights for senior officers, photographers and pressmen, in addition to participation in displays. The latter included an appearance at the 1962 Farnborough Air Show with a four-aircraft display team. In the words of the CO, 'Spiv' Leahy, 'this was a frantic time and, due to unserviceabilities, we had to borrow aircraft from 801'. However, the first appearance of the Fleet Air Arm's Buccaneers was a great success and heralded the first of countless appearances at air shows over the coming years.

The flight flew hard for the remainder of its existence, including deck trials on HMS *Hermes*. It was finally disbanded on 20 December 1962, having existed for twenty-one months instead of the twelve originally envisaged, with 1,258 hours being flown in the Buccaneer. The last word on 700Z Flight should be left to 'Spiv' Leahy:

> All pilots found the Buccaneer an easy and pleasant aircraft to fly – albeit one which required extensive ground instruction, explicit briefing and careful handling. The observers were impressed with the comprehensive navigation equipment and all aircrew enjoyed working with the weapon system. Our work was enjoyable and we believed that what we did was important. Every month we had to submit, to the world and his brother if they were cleared to SECRET, a detailed report covering every aspect of our trials but we never got a response from anyone. So, in one report, I buried in an obscure engineering section the message 'I will buy the first person to read this and contact me a pint of beer.' Forty years later nobody has rung back, so all bets are now off!
>
> During this exciting and demanding time, I don't think any of us could possibly have anticipated that the Buccaneer would have such a long and distinguished career and attract such affection from so many air and ground crews in dark and light blue.

No. 801 Squadron, commanded by Ted Anson, became the first front-line Buccaneer squadron when it was commissioned at a ceremony held at Lossiemouth on 17 July 1962 with Vice-Admiral D.P. Dreyer CB CBE DSC, the Flag Officer Air (Home), taking the salute. There was an interesting sequel to this traditional naval ceremony when Mr Tom Driberg, the Labour Member of Parliament for Barking, posed the question in the House of Commons to the Civil Lord of the Admiralty: 'What religious service took place at the commissioning ceremony at Lossiemouth of a naval aircraft designed for the delivery of hydrogen bombs . . . and does this not create a certain incongruity in the proceedings?' Mr Orr-Ewing replied: 'No, I do not think so. I think it is right to ask God's help for all those who play a gallant and dedicated part in deterring aggression and keeping the peace of this country.' This was received in the House by cheers.

No. 809 Squadron formed at Lossiemouth on 15 January 1963 under the command of the former 700Z CO, Commander 'Spiv' Leahy. The Squadron's role was to act as the Headquarters Squadron with one flight tasked to continue the trials work of 700Z and the second flight running all the conversion courses for future Buccaneer aircrew. Initially, aircrew were drawn from other Fleet Air Arm squadrons and converted to the Buccaneer after some forty hours' flying. Within twelve months the first of the less experienced and those direct from initial training arrived to commence the standard course of almost 100 hours.

An 801 Squadron S Mark 1, in the all-white anti-nuclear flash scheme with toned-down markings, taxis during the 1962 Farnborough Air Show. The aircraft has the HMS *Ark Royal* 'R' deck code on the fin and the aircraft code '119' is carried on the nose of the aircraft. (*Ian Black*)

During this first year there was also much further work required to develop the weapon system and practise the various weapon attack delivery options. For its day, the weapon system, with its associated head-up display, was very advanced and complex and it provided the heart of the weapon delivery system. Some of the aircraft allocated to 809 Squadron were the first fully capable aircraft and so much of the pioneer work to make the system operational fell to the Squadron. Central to this crucial development was Lieutenant-Commander Peter Walwyn, an observer with a Cambridge Honours degree in Electrical Engineering. He was uniquely qualified for the task and could discuss the most detailed engineering aspects and necessary modifications with the specialist engineering staff as well as flying many of the trials.

The weapon system was designed for the Buccaneer's primary attack option to deliver a nuclear bomb in a toss manoeuvre against the *Sverdlov* heavy cruiser. Peter Walwyn describes the 'long-toss' mode:

> The observer located the target at some 200 miles on the Ferranti 'Blue Parrot' radar and marked it before the aircraft descended to low level outside the lobe of the enemy radar. The aircraft approached at 550-plus kts at fifty to a hundred feet using the radio altimeter. Using the Ferranti Strike Sight Head-Up Display (HUD) the pilot steered the aircraft towards the target – the observer having entered his estimate of the target's course and speed and wind velocity to cause the aiming dot to give the pilot a nominal collision course. When the time-to-go to the target reduced to twenty-nine point five seconds (four miles) the pilot 'accepted' the attack by pressing his firing trigger, and three seconds later the strike sight caused the aiming dot to cage centrally and to precess vertically upwards at a nominal six degrees per second. By following the rising dot with the 'aim' symbol, the pilot pulled the Buccaneer into a steady 4–5 g loop during which the analogue

computer, supplemented by two accelerometers, solved the release equation. The weapon was released when the calculated forward throw equalled the horizontal distance to the target.

At the moment of release, the Buccaneer was about 60° nose up and the pilot immediately applied 135° of bank until the nose came to the horizon when the angle of bank was reduced to 90° and then further reduced to 70° and the aircraft dived for low level to complete the escape manoeuvre. Should the Blue Parrot radar fail, the pilot steered the aircraft directly over the target, 'accepting' the attack as he did so, and then completing the pull-up in the same manner as for the Long Toss mode. In this so-called 'Over the Shoulder' mode, weapon release occurred when the Buccaneer was inverted in a 70° climb at some 10,500 ft above the target!

The third computed weapon attack mode was 'Dive Toss' and, as its name suggests, it involved diving straight at the target with the radar locked on. The pull-up was commanded on the HUD when the time-to-go was 8 seconds and the bombs were released. Although extensive trials were conducted later to try and perfect this delivery mode the Buccaneer squadrons rarely used it.

No. 809 Squadron developed two new weapon delivery modes. Medium Toss was a version of Long Toss adapted for 1,000-lb HE bombs. The aircraft got closer to the target and pulled up at about 2½ miles, with the bombs released at some 30° nose up, to obtain a centre-stick hit. Recovery was completed in the same manner as Long Toss. The second new mode was Auto Depressed Sight Line (ADSL) a semi-automatic dive-bombing mode designed to improve the accuracy of 1,000-lb bomb delivery. The bomb was released in a 20° dive using a depressed sight symbol, requiring the aircraft to fly a bunted flight path. The bomb was released when approximately 0.5 g was achieved. In 20° manual

The Buccaneer representative for the Royal Review of the Fleet Air Arm held at RNAS Yeovilton on 28 May 1964 was XN 960 of 809 Squadron. The squadron badge of a Phoenix is displayed on the starboard engine cowling. Other Buccaneers in the distance are being prepared for the flypast. (*P.H.T. Green*)

dive bombing mode the pilot could be quite robust but ADSL required learning a new, very smooth, tracking technique and was very sensitive to stick 'jerks' as the 0.5 g release point was approached. However, once mastered, bombing accuracy could be surprisingly good.

In April 1965, 809 Squadron was disbanded, having carried out the role of Buccaneer Trials and Training Squadron for over two years. During this time, numerous equipment trials had been carried out and almost eighty pilots and observers had been converted to the Buccaneer. The newly commissioned 736 Squadron, commanded by Lieutenant-Commander Willie Watson, assumed the training role. With more Buccaneer squadrons entering service there was an increasing demand on the training squadron to produce more crews. Amongst the new crews joining the Buccaneer force were Flight Lieutenants Graham Smart and Graham Pitchfork, who were to be the first of a steady stream of Royal Air Force crews to complete exchange or loan postings to the Fleet Air Arm over the next thirteen years and who would form the nucleus of the future RAF Buccaneer squadrons. Also converting to the Buccaneer was Lieutenant-Commander David Howard, who had many hours flying the Seahawk and Scimitar:

> Like most naval strike/attack pilots I came from a single-seat background. Suddenly, I had someone in the back seat and for the first time in my flying career I found I was not wrestling with a large folded map in the cramped cockpit of a single-seat fighter and getting lost, so having a 'talking map' was a marvellous new experience. More importantly, having an observer gave me a tremendous amount of scope and extra flexibility to widen my thinking and tactical awareness,

XN 965 of 736 Squadron, but still displaying the 809 Squadron badge, visits RAF Scampton in September 1965. The aircraft is carrying an AGM-12 Bullpup missile on the starboard-inner pylon. The missile was not very accurate and was rarely considered for operational use. (*P.H.T. Green*)

knowing that so much was being taken care of in the back by someone with specialist knowledge and expertise. It also generated a great feeling of teamwork that was such a fundamental aspect of Buccaneer operations.

The Buccaneer was a joy to fly and the Mark 1 in particular was a superb aircraft to take to the deck. With the under-powered Gyron Juniors we had to hold a higher RPM on the approach to land, and this made the engines much more responsive than the Mark 2. You could set 87 per cent at the top of the glide path and just leave it all the way down. However, both Marks were a delight to fly from a carrier. Also, you could take the Buccaneer overland in turbulent conditions that you would not dare think of doing with others. The aircraft gave an outstandingly smooth and comfortable ride and was so stable. However, although the aircraft was doing everything it was designed to do and was way ahead in concept, it was using World War Two weapons and we had to devise our tactics around these weapons at a time when surface-to-air defences were improving rapidly, and I felt that I was flying a great aircraft that was being severely limited in what it could do because we lacked a reliable and operationally viable stand-off weapon.

The aircraft's wing fold had to allow the aircraft to be lowered on the standard-size aircraft-carrier lifts. The small size of the air intakes for the Mark 1's Gyron Junior engines is very evident. The 736 Squadron aircraft is fitted with two 430-imperial gallon wing tanks. (*David Thompson*)

For the next six years, 736 Squadron at RNAS Lossiemouth trained all Buccaneer aircrew. Pilot conversion to the Buccaneer was a challenge. Budgetary constraints had dictated that there would be no dual-control Buccaneer and the aircraft was fitted with a non-standard instrument panel, the OR 946 Integrated Flight Instrument System (IFIS). A number of dual-control Hunter T 8s were modified and equipped with the IFIS panel in the left-hand seat, and pilots flew five sorties in the Hunter prior to the first flight in a Buccaneer. Observers also flew in the Hunter on a number of low-level navigation sorties before the crew embarked on a series of Buccaneer simulator sorties. In the 1960s simulators were very basic and could best be described as cockpit and emergency procedure trainers. After five simulator sorties, and an aircrew notes and emergencies quiz, the crew were ready for their first Buccaneer sortie. The observer/navigator had the reassurance of knowing that his 'Fam 1' would be with a very experienced Buccaneer instructor pilot. The student pilot, however, climbed into the front cockpit and an even braver pilot instructor sat in the back clutching a checklist, but with no control over the aircraft whatsoever. The first Buccaneer Qualified Flying Instructor (QFI) was Bill Ryce:

The Navy decided there was a requirement for a QFI with Buccaneer experience to help with pilot training. Having spent two and a half years with 700Z Flight I was selected and left for the Central Flying School (CFS) before returning to Lossiemouth as the Buccaneer QFI on 736 Squadron. A very busy time followed. I put the pilots through the simulator course, I flew with them in a Hunter T8 that was equipped with Buccaneer instruments and when I felt they were

> ready, I sat in the back seat on their first three trips. This was too much really and I quickly reduced this to their first trip only. On one epic day in August 1964 I sat in the back seat for two Fam 1 sorties. On the first we had a hydraulic failure and on the second an engine fire which led to a single-engine landing. The student pilots handled both emergencies very well and this gave me confidence that the conversion training we had set in place, was sound. All in a day's work!

Remarkably, in thirty-five years of operations, only one aircraft was lost on a Fam 1 – and that due entirely to mechanical failure. Once five familiarisation sorties had been flown with instructors, the student pilot and observer teamed up and flew most sorties together, although the first sortie of each new phase was flown with an experienced instructor. Early flying exercises included an introduction to the weapon system and radar, followed by low-level navigation exercises, formation flying and dive-bombing. Weapons training and low-level tactical flying formed the core of the course. The designated low-flying areas in the north of Scotland provided outstanding opportunities for learning the art of low-level operations. Equally, the facilities at Tain range, just 5 minutes' flying time from Lossiemouth, were superb and all the visual and blind bombing and rocket attacks could be practised. Crews used a number of Initial Points (IPs) to enter the range, depending on the attack mode, and Lieutenant Mike Maddox remembers two in particular:

> We bombarded Tain range ceaselessly. A well-known bearded Scottish actor complained about the use of his house as an IP and so we invited him to a mess dinner, but he had an after-dinner altercation about seal-culling with another bearded Scotsman, Willie Stewert, the Lieutenant-Commander Operations. I can't remember who put whose head in the blazing wardroom fire but it didn't stop him complaining. That other long-suffering IP to Tain range – the Glen Morangie distillery – never complained. They probably recognised that we were responsible for opening up their malt whisky trade.

As the course progressed, toss bombing, photographic reconnaissance, night flying and simulated strikes were flown during the advanced phase. It was also time to learn about deck operations. However, before the first trip to an aircraft-carrier, crews practised the procedures ashore. Each crew paid a visit to the RAE airfield at Bedford to experience a catapult shot from the 'Static Steam Catapult'. Without the 30 kts of wind normally expected to blow over the deck of an aircraft-carrier, many crews thought that the Bedford catapult was more hair-raising than the real thing! It was then time to practise the art of landing safely on a very small deck. A dummy deck was marked out on the runway at Lossiemouth and a standard aircraft-carrier projector site was situated in the appropriate place on the port side. Crews then pounded the circuit, doing as many as ten MADDL (Mirror-Assisted Dummy Deck Landing) touch-and-goes per sortie before going to the deck for the first time. If a carrier was in UK waters the MADDL's phase was followed by a session of DLPs (Deck Landing Practice). For his first sortie to the deck, a student pilot had an instructor pilot in the back – the same nerveless hero who had probably just flown a first solo with a new student pilot! All pilots remember their first solo, but for naval pilots following close in the memory is their first visit to the deck of an aircraft-carrier. Sub-Lieutenant Frank Cox was just completing his Buccaneer conversion when he went to the deck for the first time and remembers the event vividly:

> I was crewed with a Kiwi observer, Noel Rawbone, who had transferred from Sea Vixens to the Buccaneer. We flew to Yeovilton for a session of DLPs (rollers), on HMS *Eagle* in Lyme Bay and these went as advertised. The CO, Lieutenant-Commander 'Willy' Watson, wrote in my log book what seemed to me to be a major understatement 'Two sorties of DLP in HMS *Eagle* satisfactory and safe'. Anything that was not dangerous or life-

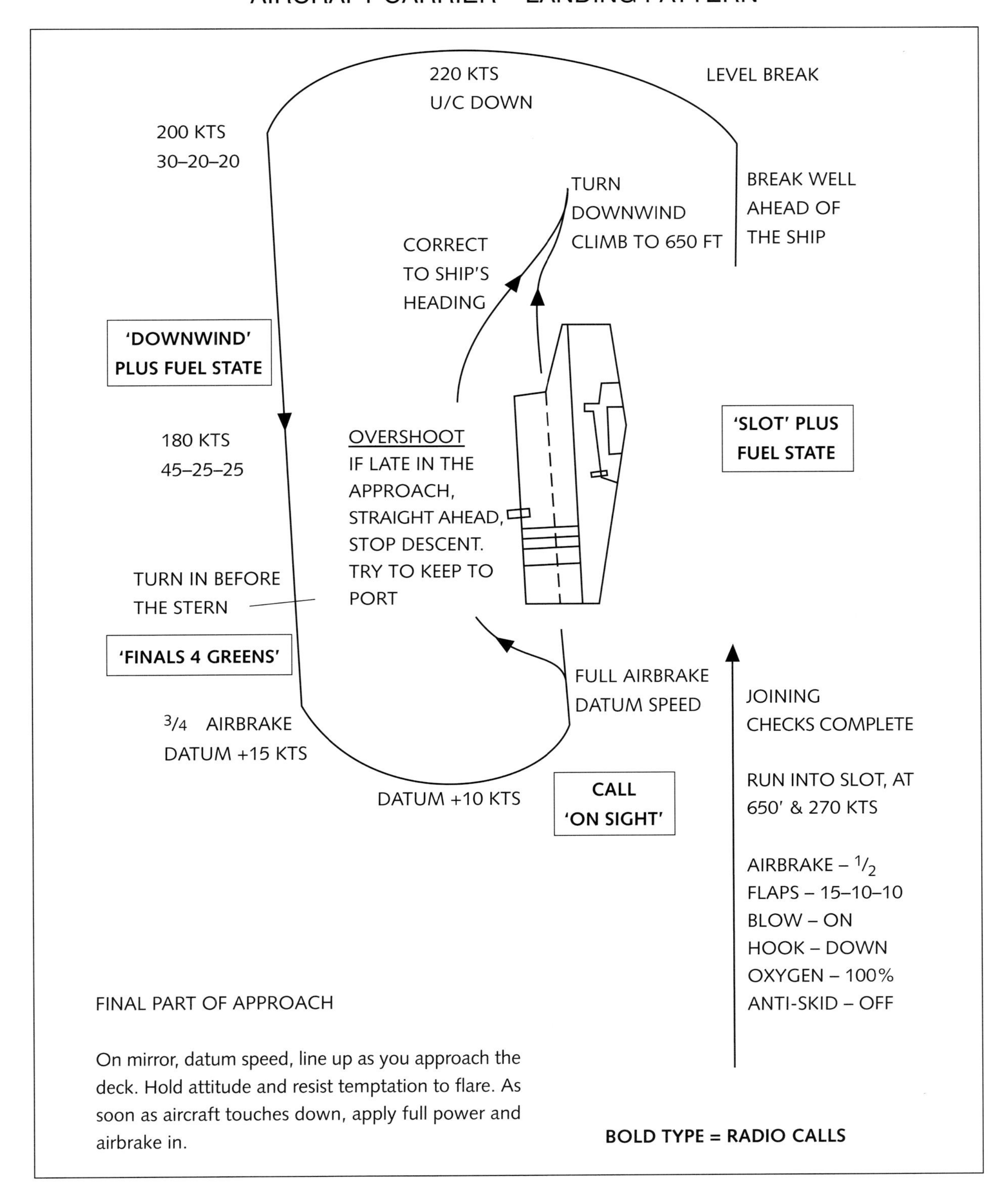

This diagram formed part of the initial briefing given to all aircrews before they visited the deck of an aircraft-carrier for the first time.

The instructors of 736 Squadron practise formation aerobatics over the Moray Firth in February 1967. The Squadron's first S Mark 2, XT 275, is flying in the number four 'box' position. The photograph illustrates the larger air intakes needed for the Rolls Royce Spey-engined aircraft and the more pointed wing tips. (*Author*)

threatening must have been OK! I then joined 800 Squadron and soon afterwards we flew to the carrier and I carried out two DLPs. As we were passing the bow on the second of these, Wings called 'hook down' and suddenly the cosiness of the cockpit was lost and the adrenalin started to flow. Noel, who had experienced many landings from the 'coal-hole' during his Sea Vixen days, was lifted from his boredom and laconically mentioned that this would be the first time he could see what was going on during and after a landing. We turned finals and gave the straps a final tighten. For some reason I seemed to be making a lot more control inputs than previously but we hit the deck, caught a wire and came to a shuddering halt with me still trying to comprehend what had happened. The next recollection is of Noel expressing his happiness at having arrived in one piece but urging me to watch the marshaller immediately in front who was indicating that I should get a move on, raise the hook, fold the wings, put the power on, taxi ahead and turn right. Parking on deck was an eye-opener for the first time, and I must have been timid because the 'come ahead' signals from the marshaller were getting more earnest the closer we got to the edge of the deck up in the bow, where I had already lost sight of the deck and could only see the sea ahead of me. I had no idea which wire I caught but was just happy to have landed more or less in the right place.

After discovering the mysteries of air-to-air refuelling, the final exercise on the conversion course was flown. This 'Opex' consisted of a simulated operational strike sortie culminating in an attack with practice weapons at Tain or Rosehearty ranges. For the first few years, 736 Squadron was equipped with the Mark 1, but once all the front-line Buccaneer squadrons were equipped with the Mark 2, students completed five conversion sorties to the Mark 2 before joining their squadrons.

Not all sorties went according to plan, and Bill Ryce experienced one of the most dramatic:

Late in November 1965 I was the duty officer when Air Traffic rang and asked me to arrange a weather check to the north of the Moray Firth to see if any more snow was heading our way. Earlier in the day, snow clearance had been started but was stopped due to the bad weather and they wanted to know if it was worth restarting. I checked the runway conditions and phoned back to say that Runway 29 was unfit for operations. The second, rather apologetic, call from Air Traffic passed on the message that the request for a weather check was not a 'request'. Such is life!

I decided to make the flight myself and Trevor Ling, a trainee Observer, joined me. The aircraft was sliding all over the place as we taxied out and, with some difficulty, we got lined up on the runway and started a rolling take-off as the brakes would not hold the aircraft stationary when power was applied. I had briefed Trevor that if we abandoned the take-off I would drop the hook and hopefully we would take the wire. With some relief we got airborne but problems started immediately.

When I selected the undercarriage up, we had a total AC electrical failure and the back-up supply also failed – so I lost all the cockpit instruments. There was some external noise, which I could not place, and apparently this was the nose wheel that had slewed sideways and jammed against the fuselage (no cockpit indication). It transpired that we had lost most of our hydraulics, including both main systems and one flying control system.

I levelled off at about 2,000 ft and turned right, over the sea, planning to recover back on to Runway 29. What worried me as I was trying to sort things out was the lack of a common thread to the problems I was experiencing and I was half expecting something catastrophic to happen next. It went through my mind that shards of ice, thrown up during the take-off may have damaged the electric cables in the wheel wells but I was too busy to dwell on that. I looked over at the airfield and the icy runway did not look very inviting but it looked considerably better than the grey Moray Firth below us. I lowered the undercarriage and got reassuring noises, but no cockpit indications, so I asked Air Traffic to do a visual check. They replied that all three legs looked down, so I decided to land. I had no idea of my flap/droop/airbrake situation so speed control on the approach was a bit of a problem and I was basically flying by 'feel'. I told Trevor that if I called 'eject' it was not a subject for discussion!

On finals, the controls felt pretty slack so it was with a sense of relief that I put the aircraft down on the end of the runway. I was aware of a bit of sliding, which I expected, but then I felt the left wing dropping which I was not expecting. I held the wing up as long as I could but as we lost aerodynamic lift, down it went and we started curving over the grass to the left. I was mindful all the time that Trevor was a student, but he was very helpful throughout the short flight and got rid of the canopy as we were doing our tractor imitation. It transpired that the left undercarriage leg was not locked down.

Bill Ryce was the Buccaneer QFI and simulator instructor, so he was very familiar with the aircraft systems and had inflicted countless emergency situations on the trainee crews. However, he admitted that the emergencies he was confronted with were well beyond any sequence of problems that he could have dreamed up. His many students were not slow to remind him that this incident had been payback time; it could not have happened to a better person – the biter bit! This was undoubtedly one of the most alarming emergencies encountered in the Buccaneer era but there was no one more qualified to rescue such a desperate situation than Bill Ryce. He was awarded a Green Endorsement for his 'outstanding professionalism and skill'.

The training routine for 736 Squadron was interrupted on Tuesday 28 March 1967. The day had started as another routine day of training flying at RNAS Lossiemouth, but dramatic events soon unfolded. After recovering the first morning sorties, 736 and 800 Squadrons were told to stand by, ready to bomb the *Torrey Canyon* with 1,000-lb HE bombs. The 118,000-ton supertanker had run aground on the Seven Stones Reef, 16 miles from Land's End, ten days earlier, and all attempts to tow her free had failed. With the tanker starting to leak oil and break up, it was decided to minimise the risk of massive pollution of the coastline by destroying the tanker and firing the escaping oil. Eight Buccaneers of the two Lossiemouth squadrons were tasked to 'open up' the tanker, and bomb-loading teams were soon in action. As soon as aircraft were bombed up they took off in pairs throughout the afternoon. Leading the attack was the Commanding Officer of 736 Squadron, David Howard:

> The weather was good when we arrived and we circled round once to decide the best line of attack, which we decided should be made from the direction of the Scilly Isles. I went down first in a 20° dive and one of my bombs hit the starboard side but failed to explode. Dave Mears, the Senior Pilot of 800 Squadron, who scored two direct hits in the middle of the stern section starting a fierce fire, followed me in. On my next run, I dropped two bombs on target and there was so much flame and smoke it was difficult to see anything of the stern section. By this time, the burning oil was spreading very fast over the sea. It got worse as we pumped more bombs in and the smoke got very black and dense and we had to alter our line of attack to avoid flying through the smoke. I was also rather worried in case the tanker blew up. During the attack we went in singly and took our time about it and 75 per cent of the bombs were on target.

During the afternoon three more pairs of Buccaneers added their weight of bombs to the burning tanker. Last on the scene were Lieutenant Jonathon Tod and the author, who saw the rising

On 28 March 1967, Buccaneers of 736 and 800 Squadrons bombed the grounded tanker *Torrey Canyon* with 1,000-lb HE bombs. No. 736 Squadron used both Mark 1 and 2 aircraft with one of each seen being re-armed at RNAS Brawdy. Bombs have been loaded on the inner pylons and others have been prepared for hoisting in to the open bomb bay, which carried four. The different sized engine air intakes are very apparent. (*Peter Mathews*)

smoke as they flew southwards over Bristol. By this time the Chivenor-based Hunters had added their 'fire bombs' to the burning oil, so choosing a line of attack for the 20° dive-bombing attacks was difficult, but successful drops were made, including a bomb down the funnel of the stricken tanker. Over the next two days further attacks by other Fleet Air Arm and RAF aircraft were carried out, including sixteen by the 736 and 800 Squadron Buccaneers using RNAS Brawdy for refuelling and re-arming. By the end of the operation the wreck was hardly visible and oil had ceased to flow. The operation against the *Torrey Canyon* was mounted with virtually no notice and no preparation and it was a tribute to the professionalism of the air and ground crews of the two squadrons. Special mention has to be made of the incredible efforts of the armourers, many still under training with 736 Squadron, who prepared and loaded over 100 live 1,000-lb bombs without respite over three days. In addition to the Royal Navy aircrews, two RAF men flew on the first day, and the Buccaneer airborne tanker supporting the Mark 1s of 736 Squadron was flown by a French Navy pilot and a US Navy observer. Summing up the operation, one squadron wag commented: 'Just my sort of target. Massive, stationary, perfect weather and not firing back!'

After this unexpected interlude, 736 Squadron was soon back training crews for the front-line squadrons. Many had just completed flying training and the Buccaneer was a huge step forward. The failure rate was remarkably small and a testament to the standard of instruction and the skill of the aircrews. Sub-Lieutenant Tony Ogilvy was a young pilot direct from training and he has captured the feelings of all those who flew the Buccaneer:

> I was totally hooked on the Buccaneer from Day One. With nothing to fall back on in the way of experience, and only the Hunter to compare (all of 150 hours), it mattered not one jot that the aircraft needed a bit of delicate handling in the dirty configuration. You just accepted that as a small price to pay for the most incomparable handling qualities below 1,000 ft. The conversion on 736 Squadron was excellent, with a team of top instructors who really enthused about the aircraft. I did the first half of the course on the Mark 1, and although it was a bit short on overall power, I had no particular problems or gripes with the Gyron Juniors. The Mark 2 was a whole new ball game of course, and, once used to the engine response from the high bypass ratio Spey engines, we never looked back. This was truly a formidable attack aircraft. We all recognised it as a world-beater, and flying it as a brand new Sub-Lieutenant of twenty-one was an unforgettable experience that I can recall to this day.
>
> I recognised early on in my flying career that the only place to operate, and really feel operational, was below 1,000 ft. Fortunately we had the north Scotland low-flying area, and guys in the back – instructors or constituted crew – who felt the same. The whole *raison d'être* of approaching and attacking at minimum height drove all our thinking, tactical application and safety patterns and this was inculcated from Day One – and I lapped it up. It was particularly striking that the instructors were quite often pushing student pilots to get lower, hold the line, don't balloon over skylines etc. After years of restrictive coaching (quite rightly) in the advanced flying training courses, we were suddenly let off the leash, but in a measured and safe environment that allowed us to develop as individuals the vital skills in operating at low level, and with a buddy in the back as the team. I thoroughly enjoyed the two-seat concept and could never understand why some chose to hark back with pleasure to single-seat operations.
>
> The spirit amongst the mixed RN/RAF crews was surely what military *esprit de corps* was meant to be. Why am I still eager to get to the Blitz [annual reunion] every year, along with all the others? Simple: we knew we were the best then, and still think that way now.

Before converting to the Sea Harrier twelve years later, Tony Ogilvy had amassed more than 2,000 hours on the Buccaneer and was the Royal Navy's senior air warfare instructor on the Buccaneer.

CHAPTER 3

Carrier Operations

No. 801 Squadron was the first Buccaneer squadron to operate at sea. The Squadron's work-up included four weeks embarked in HMS *Ark Royal*, when the pilots had their first experience of flying the Buccaneer from the deck. On 12 August 1963 the Squadron embarked in HMS *Victorious* with ten aircraft and sailed for the Far East. After a fast passage to the Indian Ocean the ship commenced a concentrated work-up period before embarking on a long and very varied commission that took the squadron to all the traditional naval ports east of Suez. In addition, they also conducted various weapon delivery trials including the first firing of the Bullpup anti-ship missile. It was also the period of confrontation with Indonesia and Mike Maddox, a squadron observer and Electronic Warfare Instructor (EWI), remembers the first cruise:

> Having come from a tour on Sea Vixens I found the Mark One a bit pedestrian being very underpowered. I remember offending my navigation instructor by suggesting that I could prepare the flight plan while rolling down the runway waiting for lift off! The Gyron Junior engine gasped for air and the inlet guide vanes constantly banged when a small amount of 'g' was pulled at high level. As EWI, I had great fun with the Wide Band Homer [a threat-radar warning receiver], which was a backseater's chance to get his own back on the pilots. I never forget one night

Two Buccaneer S 1s of 801 Squadron tensioned on the catapults of HMS *Victorious*. The aircraft on the starboard catapult is about to be launched and the aircraft on the port catapult is already tensioned ready for take-off within 30 seconds. The hold-back is clearly visible at the rear of the aircraft. (*Peter Mathews*)

amongst the towering CuNimbs, recording Indonesian (Soviet) radars, when there was the unmistakable 'beep-beep, beep-beep' of an airborne interception radar operating in S-band. I told my pilot, Jack Smith, that it must be a MiG-19 and he should urgently check his six o'clock, which he did for some time – resulting in a very stiff neck. In due course, a Tengah-based Javelin came alongside!

The second front-line squadron, 800, was commissioned at Lossiemouth on 18 March 1964 under the command of Lieutenant-Commander Chris Mather. After a work-up period, the Squadron embarked in HMS *Eagle* in Lyme Bay on 2 December 1964, before making a fast passage to Aden. Following the decommissioning of 809 Squadron and the return to the United Kingdom of 801 Squadron, 800 continued the various weapon delivery trials, in particular the medium-toss and ADSL modes. Peter Walwyn joined the squadron off Singapore to assist with those trials:

The squadron flew a number of medium-toss sorties dropping the 1,000-lb bomb against the US Navy's quarter-mile-square island target, which had a radar reflector. The 'fall of shot' spotting was done from the mainland, about a mile away! First the radar locked-on mode and, secondly, the Doppler-stabilised target marker computer mode using a lighthouse as an initial point some 12 miles from the target. The latter method was the most likely against any potential Indonesian airfield targets. The object of these flights was to compare the accuracy of the two different modes.

Pull-up was initiated at about 3 miles, flying at 550 kts, and every run produced a call of 'Hit' from the range safety officer until Chris Mather asked in

The nose wheel of this 801 Squadron Buccaneer failed to lock down and the pilot, Lieutenant Nick Wilkinson, was confronted with landing into the safety barrier on HMS *Victorious* during flying exercises off Subic Bay in the Philippines in June 1964. The recovery party are hard at work to clear the deck. (*Peter Mathews*)

Buccaneer S 1, XN 962, tosses eight 1,000-lb bombs, four from the bomb bay and two from each wing. The bombs were given different markings in order to assess the release timings and spacing. (*Author*)

exasperation 'Hit what?' Back came the reply 'the island'. Clearly they were used to US Navy accuracies!! Scores were subsequently passed as a clock-code and range, and they were gratifyingly small for both modes. Following 800 Squadron's successful assessment the two new modes were adopted by all future Buccaneer squadrons.

The trials also highlighted the marginal take-off performance provided by the Gyron Junior engines of the Mark 1. Operating from the deck in high temperatures, any lack of wind over the deck presented the aircrew with some exciting moments. The engines' inlet guide vanes (IGVs) had a tendency to stall under certain conditions, causing loud bangs to emanate from the offending engine – an uncomfortable feeling as the Flight Deck Officer stood poised to drop his green flag as a signal to catapult the aircraft off the deck. A quick flick of the boundary layer control (BLC) switch was often enough to unstall the IGVs and the engine picked up to provide its very modest maximum thrust. However, loaded with a full complement of eight 1,000-lb bombs, the aircraft could only take off with half fuel and, immediately after launch, it joined up with a Scimitar tanker of 800B Flight and air-to-air refuelled to full. Although the Mark 1 was underpowered, pilots soon recognised that the Buccaneer was an outstanding aircraft.

Flying operations from the deck of a fully worked-up aircraft-carrier require considerable skill and precision from both the aircrew and the deck party of engineers, maintenance ratings, controllers, marshallers and catapult crews. On a routine day the first wave of sorties took off at six o'clock in the morning with four Buccaneers programmed together with a spare, which was manned and started in case one of the four became unserviceable. Briefing for the five crews started an hour before the launch and, after donning the numerous items of flying clothing, the crews signed the aircraft's Form 700 and walked on deck to their aircraft. The ship steamed slowly downwind as the order to 'start the Buccaneers' was passed over the ship's broadcast system by Flying Control (Flyco). After engine start and completion of the challenge-and-response pre-flight and pre-launch checks, the rendezvous lights on the upper and lower fuselage were switched on to signify to Flyco that the aircraft was serviceable for the launch. An important part of the pre-launch check was to secure the oxygen mask, select oxygen to 100 per cent and to close the canopy before taxiing on deck. This gave the crew the best possible chances of escape should the aircraft slide off the deck during taxiing. Equally important was a quick check of the brakes as the aircraft started to taxi to the catapult. As the aircraft prepared to launch, the Wessex SAR helicopter took off and hovered reassuringly alongside the port side of the carrier with its diver sitting in the doorway ready to drop into the sea and effect a rescue.

During the Mark 1 days, the Buccaneers were the last to launch after the completion of the Sea Vixen launch and they taxied forward to the bow or waist catapult as they spread their wings. The nose-wheel steering system of the Buccaneer was excellent and allowed very precise taxiing to the catapult under the meticulous direction of the aircraft marshaller. The aircraft was lined up with the catapult groove and taxied forward to the rollers that ensured that it was centred on the catapult, with the main wheels against the retractable chocks. The blast deflector plates were raised and the armament safety breaks connected by the maintenance ratings, as the aircrew placed their hands on top of their helmets. Meanwhile, the shuttle travelled down the catapult to a position just behind the nose-wheel. The catapult crew attached the holdback to the deck and the heavy 2-in-gauge wire strop to the front of the shuttle and the two-eyed ends were attached to the hooks on either side of the fuselage. The shuttle was moved forward to tension the strop and the Buccaneer nose was lifted to the take-off position. The aircrew calculated the tail-plane trim setting and this was checked visually by the

Aircrews man their aircraft ready to launch from HMS *Eagle*. Five Buccaneers of 800 Squadron were prepared but only four launched, the fifth acting as a spare if one became unserviceable. The two Scimitar tankers of 800B Flight were launched before the Buccaneers and later they joined up to refuel the Buccaneers. The carrier is about to increase speed and turn into wind for the launch as the frigate positions on the port quarter to act as the plane guard. (*Author*)

This Buccaneer S 1 of 800 Squadron is about to be launched from the waist catapult of HMS *Eagle*. The aircraft is tensioned and the blast deflector is in the raised position. The Flight Deck Officer has his green flag raised and is just waiting for the pilot to signal that he is ready to accept the launch. (*Author*)

squadron engineering officer against a graduated quadrant at the top of the fin. In the meantime, the catapult officer in his small glass-sided cell at the edge of the deck calculated the end speed required, and thus the necessary steam pressure, based on the aircraft's all-up weight and the wind-over-the-deck component. Once the catapult chief was satisfied that the aircraft was properly loaded he waved away the deck parties and handed over to the Flight Deck Officer (FDO), who raised a green flag and waved it above his head, giving the cue for the pilot to apply full power and complete the final pre-launch checks of sufficient engine thrust and blow pressure for the drooped flaps, ailerons and tail plane. Once the pilot was happy, he placed the back of his hand against the starboard quarter canopy. The FDO then checked with Flyco and, once satisfied, lowered the green flag to the deck and the catapult was fired. A Buccaneer catapult launch was carried out with the pilot's 'hands off' and, after a ride down the catapult lasting just over one second, the Buccaneer was airborne at 140 knots and the strop fell away into the sea. Had the pilot been unhappy to launch he would have maintained full power and shaken his head from side to side and the FDO would have raised his red flag and kept both flags up until the catapult officer had cancelled the launch. A few seconds after the first Buccaneer had successfully launched, the second followed and within 2 minutes a second pair were launched. Frank Cox recalls his first catapult take-off:

> The catapult at RAE Bedford, where hapless students usually experienced their first cat shot with plenty of runway in front in case things went awry, had been unserviceable for months. Hence, my first launch came just after I was getting over the shock of my first arrival on deck the day before. The preparation and loading on the catapult were not a problem, except I found the motion of the ship somewhat disconcerting. The tensioning procedure as it hoisted the aircraft into the flying attitude raised the blood pressure somewhat, but nothing had prepared me for what was to follow. I signalled the flight deck officer that we had completed the checks and were ready, he dropped his green flag and I was just preparing myself for the event when it happened! Nothing on this earth equates to the experience of the first 'cat shot'. I remember my observer reminding me that I should be getting the gear and flaps up after what was a mind-numbing

ride which had left my brain sitting well behind the tail. However, as I was soon to discover, all subsequent launches were a pleasure and the easiest way by far to get airborne.

An hour after the launch, the recovery back on board commenced. At the morning brief each pair of aircraft would be given a 'Charlie' time (the time to arrive in the waiting area prior to making an approach to land) and a minimum approach fuel state. Once established in the wait on the port quarter at 1,500 ft, each pair was called by Flyco to 'slot' as the ship turned onto the Designated Flying Course (DFC) and increased speed to 25 kts. Approaching the 'slot' abeam the island on the starboard side, the Buccaneers slowed to 270 kts at 600 ft with the hook down and completed the pre-joining checks, which included selecting the 15-10-10 flap and aileron configuration with the blow switched on. A level break was carried out well ahead of the ship to allow plenty of time downwind and, as the speed decayed to 220 kts, the undercarriage was lowered and the next stage of flap selected. The 'downwind' call was made, together with the fuel state, and the crew calculated the landing datum speed based on the aircraft's all-up weight. Once abeam the stern of the ship, with a speed of datum plus 15 kts and half airbrake out, the turn on to finals was made with the radio call of 'sight, four greens'. As the aircraft approached the ship's wake the pilot picked up the 'meatball' on the projector site, situated on the port side, and the remainder of the airbrake was eased out and throttle adjustments made to remain on the glide slope. Pilots aimed to line up as soon as possible and then concentrate on maintaining the correct glide slope and speed, which was presented on a precision deck landing ASI placed in a prominent position on the cockpit coaming, together with an audible prompting of the Airflow Direction Detector (ADD) heard over the crew's headsets. A Projector Sight Officer – later called the Landing Safety Officer (LSO) – was positioned at the projector sight to give advice and, under certain circumstances, he would 'talk' the pilot down. This was particularly important at night. If the approach was poor the pilot was expected to overshoot and go for another attempt or the LSO could give the pilot a 'wave off' and instruct him to make another approach. A good approach was continued and, as the aircraft came over the ship's stern, the attitude was held with no attempt to flare the aircraft. As the wheels thumped onto the deck full power was applied and the airbrakes selected in, and almost immediately came an impressive deceleration from 130 knots to zero in a few feet. If the aircraft had missed the wires, overshoot action had already been started by the application of full power, Flyco would fire two red flares and call 'bolter,' and the crew would re-join the circuit and make another attempt. Having successfully landed, and as soon as the aircraft came to a stop, the brakes were released allowing the aircraft to roll back a short distance to disengage the wire when the hook was selected up. The wings were then folded as the pilot followed the marshaller's instructions implicitly and taxied into 'Fly One' in the bow of the ship. This was a very speedy and slick operation as the next aircraft was aiming to land on at an interval of just thirty seconds.

In normal circumstances, a crew was given two or three attempts to get on board, but once 'chicken' fuel had been reached, the aircraft was directed ashore to land at the diversion airfield and return to the ship later in the day. Night recoveries were always conducted off a Carrier Controlled Approach (CCA), when a controller talked the crew down before instructing them to look up at 400 ft and take over visually on the projector sight, assisted by advice from the reassuring LSO. On a very black night all the crew would see on an approach would be a string

The aircraft has caught number four wire and is slightly off the centre line. A member of the deck party is rushing forward to signal to the pilot to release the brakes to allow the aircraft to roll back, enabling the hook to be retracted before the aircraft taxies forward to clear the deck prior to the next aircraft landing 30 seconds behind. The Landing Safety Officer is viewing proceedings. (*Author*)

of lights marking the centre line of the angled landing area and the projector sight. The observer could see the standby sight on the starboard side and they became very adept at assessing the likely success of the approach. It was all exciting stuff and soon made boys into men. Sub-Lieutenant Dave Thompson, later to become one of the Fleet Air Arm's most experienced observers, remembers his early days at sea:

> I joined 800 Squadron during a period when they were flying from RAF Changi and, shortly afterwards, came my first deck landing on *Eagle* sailing off Singapore. My pilot and I had never seen an aircraft-carrier before and I found it almost impossible to read out the deck-landing checks and calculate the datum speed as I stared at the tiny platform that we were supposed to land on! To our delight we made it and, once we had gained some experience, came the first night launches and recoveries. First we carried out a number of dusk sorties, which generated some 'bolters' [missed the wires] with subsequent diversions to local airfields and then it was time for our first night sortie and in the Far East the nights are very black! Like most other backseaters I spoke to, I was never very happy during the last 200 feet of a night approach, hoping that my driver was in the groove and knew more about what was going on than me.

In August 1965, 800 Squadron embarked in HMS *Eagle* for a twelve-month cruise that would see the ship spending record times at sea. Not long after entering the Mediterranean for a six-week work-up, the carrier was ordered to proceed through the Suez Canal with all speed, to reinforce the British Forces in Aden after the Governor had suspended the constitution following serious civil disturbances. The

Buccaneers flew close air support sorties over the Radfan and long-range photographic reconnaissance sorties in the north of the Aden Protectorate using the Scimitar air-to-air refuelling tankers of 800B Flight to extend their range.

After a spell off Aden, HMS *Eagle* was due to replace HMS *Ark Royal* off Singapore and provide carrier-based aircraft in support of the continuing conflict with Indonesia. The Indonesian Navy's Soviet-built *Komar* fast patrol boats, armed with surface-to-surface missiles, posed a major threat with their night hit-and-run tactics. Armed with pods of 2-in rockets, the Buccaneers were tasked to take on these formidable targets. Whilst off Aden it was decided to develop and practise tactics, using an RAF Air Sea Rescue launch towing a 'splash' target at high speed, to simulate a *Komar*.

After a night launch from *Eagle*, three Buccaneers joined up in radar trail at four-mile intervals. The leader was armed with eight 'Gloworm' high-intensity flares, mounted in the head of an old 3-in rocket. A Gannet was used to identify the 'target' and provide direction for the Buccaneer formation. At three miles the leader pulled up and in a 30° climb fired the rockets in ripple, starting to bank the aircraft as the first fired in order to 'fan' the flares. In the meantime, the trailing Buccaneers turned outwards for 40 seconds and pulled up to 2,000 ft, (by which time the flares were meant to have ignited over the target) before they rolled into a 10° dive and fired off their four pods, each containing thirty-six rockets. Unfortunately, the Gloworm serviceability record was poor and many failed, either by not igniting or burning the parachute and sending a few million candle-power in free fall towards the target. Frank Cox was the pilot on one of these early trial sorties:

> I was flying one of the rocket-firing aircraft on a practice anti-FPB attack at night off Aden and maintaining four miles radar trail on the flare aircraft. As the leader called 'pulling up' I turned outwards and started a climb to 2,000 feet and had just rolled in to the dive when the flares ignited. To my consternation, there was a huge super-tanker directly below the flares and some had candled and were dropping rapidly towards the ship. We scattered. The de-brief with the Gannet crew in the Wardroom bar after we had landed back on board was interesting!

Frank Cox and his colleagues did not realise that oil tankers would soon become their major concern. After the Rhodesian Prime Minister, Ian Smith, had declared unilateral independence in November 1965, an international trade embargo was introduced and the United Nations authorised the use of force to prevent oil tankers carrying oil to Beira, the seaward terminal of the oil pipeline to Rhodesia. After patrolling in the Mozambique Channel at the end of the year, HMS *Eagle* returned in March to impose the embargo. For the next two months the Buccaneer crews of 800 Squadron flew hundreds of hours,

Sub-Lieutenants Dave Thompson and Frank Cox about to man their 800 Squadron aircraft, which has the low-pressure air starting Palouste already connected to the starboard engine. Some thirteen years later, this very youthful-looking crew were the Senior Observer and Senior Pilot of 809 Squadron and had over 4,000 Buccaneer hours and more than 1,000 deck landings between them. (*David Thompson*)

finding and monitoring the movements of all shipping within a 500-mile radius of Beira, in the search for any tankers intending to break the blockade. The Buccaneer bomb bay was capable of carrying a photographic pack containing six F95 cameras arranged as a vertical fan of three, with a further three as forward and sideways obliques. These were loaded into four aircraft and were used extensively to photograph the oil tankers sailing through the area of operations. In order to cover the largest possible areas of sea, the range of the Buccaneers had to be extended. Instrumental in identifying fuel-saving measures and devising tactics was David Howard, the Senior Pilot of 800 Squadron, who flew many sorties throughout the patrol:

> To gain more range we pored over the published range and endurance figures for the aircraft and they proved remarkably accurate, and so we could plan to return with the exact amount of recovery fuel, 3,000 lb. Of course, we were operating throughout without a diversion airfield, which could sometimes be a bit testing if there was a big swell; but we always had a clear deck for landing so did not require extra fuel to wait. The wing weapon pylons were removed to reduce drag and we became experts at balancing the fuel between tanks and using the throttles smoothly. We all became so fuel conscious that we devised our own 'how-gowzit' and always returned with the exact amount of recovery fuel.
>
> We flew three basic profiles. The first was a dawn and dusk 'lo-lo' to catch any ships creeping close along the coast. The standard profile was to fly out low level down the main shipping lane to about 300 miles before turning for the ship and climbing to high level, recording every ship and photographing tankers. Finally, there was the maximum range sortie departing at high level and in-flight refuelling from a Scimitar – in a shallow dive – before descending to low level about 550 miles from the ship and sweeping back to 300 miles before climbing to return. In this way we covered all the ships that could make Beira in the next twenty-four hours. To some it might seem unexciting, but everyone felt a great sense of achievement and we flew the aircraft to its limits, which was very rewarding.

The Buccaneers of 800 Squadron flew these profiles for forty-two consecutive days, generating 260 sorties and over 400 hours for the loss of one aircraft, which had an engine failure on finals, with the crew ejecting successfully. During this period, two oil tankers endeavoured to break the blockade and the Buccaneers photographed both. As HMS *Eagle* steamed back to Singapore after seventy-one days at sea, the Squadron diarist captured the mood: 'We have gone from better to best in flying the Buccaneer from the deck, and it will be some time before a strike squadron approaches the figures again. It must be remembered, as well, that it was all non-diversion flying.'

As 800 Squadron was using the Mark 1 to its maximum capability the much more powerful Mark 2 was being introduced into service by 700B Flight, commanded by Commander 'Freddie' Mills, and commissioned at Lossiemouth in April 1965. The Rolls Royce Spey 101 engines, each producing 11,400 lb of thrust, replaced the underpowered Gyron Junior engines and take-off problems were cured at a stroke. The fuel consumption of the Spey was much more efficient and the range of the Buccaneer improved dramatically and was amply demonstrated by long-range simulated strikes flown from Lossiemouth to Iceland and a non-stop unrefuelled flight of 1,950 miles from Goose Bay in Labrador back to Lossiemouth. In addition to the engine change, a new and more reliable and powerful electrical system was fitted, and changes to components and systems were also introduced, eliminating many of the troublesome areas of the Mark 1. Lieutenant Rob Woodard was one of the first pilots to fly the Mark 2:

> I was sent back from 801 Squadron in the Far East to join 700B, the Mark 2 Trials Flight. It was a great boost to my ego when I discovered there were only six pilots; the CO, Senior Pilot, Air Warfare Instructor and two graduates of the Empire Test

Pilots' School. I was the only non-specialist pilot. Then I discovered my selection was on the premise that if I could fly it, anyone could! The Mark 2 was a very different beast with almost twice the thrust. Deck landings required a different technique, getting the speed back early and living on power. The other great feature was its considerably increased radius of action.

As 700B proved during their intensive trials, the Mark 2 was a much more capable and reliable aircraft and the first operational squadron was commissioned just six months after the formation of the trials Flight, which decommissioned at the end of September 1965.

The first operational Buccaneer S Mark 2 squadron was formed on 14 October 1965 when 801 Squadron, under the command of Lieutenant-Commander John de Winton, was re-commissioned at Lossiemouth by Vice-Admiral Sir Richard Smeeton KCB MBE, the Flag Officer Naval Air Command. The squadron commenced an intensive work-up period, which included Bullpup missile firing and embarked flying from HMS *Victorious*. During this latter period Lieutenant John Cross and his observer, Lieutenant-Commander George Oxley, provided a graphic demonstration of the capability of the new Mark 2s. They were launched from the carrier off the Cornwall coast on 3 June 1966 and climbed on a southerly heading to rendezvous with a Buccaneer tanker. They refuelled to full over the Bay of Biscay and headed for Gibraltar, where they made a low-level pass before climbing to height and returning to the carrier and landing on after a flight of almost five hours. Such a performance made the 800 Squadron crews operating off Beira at the same time understandably envious.

With more thrust and acceleration, the initial catapult launches with the Mark 2 were very encouraging. However, once 801 Squadron started to fly long-range sorties with wing tanks fitted, a series of pitch-up problems were

An 801 Squadron Buccaneer S 2 launches from the port catapult of HMS *Victorious* in 1966. The launch was made 'hands off' and the pilot took control as the aircraft left the catapult at 140 kts, achieved in less than 2 seconds. (*Tom Eeles*)

experienced, including the loss of XN 979 immediately after a catapult launch. The crew ejected safely and the initial reason for the accident was attributed to 'pilot error', although this was overturned later. At this stage it had not been appreciated that the slightly different wing plan-form and mass distribution of the Mark 2 had a significant aerodynamic effect in certain launch configurations, in particular those with wing tanks fitted.

Further pitch-up problems occurred and an exchange of views between 801 Squadron and the Naval Test Squadron at A&AEE Boscombe Down took place, resulting in the latter suggesting that pilots were adopting the wrong technique, but problems continued. In October 1966, Lieutenant-Commander David Eagles, the senior pilot on the Naval Test Squadron, visited HMS *Victorious* and gave a talk to the aircrew of 801 Squadron, explaining the 'hands off' launch technique. He followed this with a test flight in XV 153 in the configuration that the Squadron claimed was the most vulnerable to pitch-up. The Squadron's only non-Royal Navy observer, Flight Lieutenant Colin Scriven, found himself 'volunteered' as the observer for the test flight, and the rest of the aircrew assembled above the Gun Direction Platform (GDP) to witness the event. The aircraft was boosted from the catapult for a flight that lasted barely 30 seconds! Pitch-up occurred immediately after launch and the crew ejected successfully and were recovered on board within minutes. Boscombe Down staff admitted that there was a problem.

After a series of hastily arranged trials, a number of modifications were introduced to allow catapult launches without wing tanks. A new attitude indicator gave more accurate pitch indications and there was a better tailplane position indicator. More accurate markings were incorporated on the fin to confirm this position and a revised set of tables to calculate the position were produced. After a further series of trials, the wing tanks were modified by removing the drag-reducing but lift-generating 'pen nib' fairing on top of the tank. Once all these modifications had been incorporated, the Mark 2 suffered no further problems on catapult launch.

One of the blackest and saddest days in the great history of the Fleet Air Arm occurred on 22 February 1966, when the Labour Government announced that CVA 01, the next generation of fixed-wing carrier, was to be cancelled. The second of the Mark 2 squadrons (809 commanded by Lieutenant-Commander Lyn Middleton) had just formed and 800 Squadron was re-equipping with the Mark 2. Other squadrons were due to enter service in the near future to give the Fleet Air Arm a very potent and capable strike/attack force. With Denis Healey's announcement, all this was thrown into doubt, with a consequent difficulty in recruiting enough aircrew to man the squadrons for the ten years' remaining in-service life of the current carriers. To fill the vacancies, an increasing number of RAF aircrew were loaned to the Fleet Air Arm. This measure, established at a time of adversity, was to establish one of the enduring and most significant aspects of the Buccaneer fraternity, cooperation, friendships and mutual respect that exist to this day. One of the early RAF pilots to be 'volunteered' for a loan posting was an experienced Hunter pilot, Flight-Lieutenant Peter Sturt, who remembers his introduction to the art of carrier flying:

> Almost as soon as I had completed my abbreviated conversion course to the Buccaneer I joined 809 Squadron who were disembarked at Halfar in Malta. I had never seen a deck before, not even the one marked out on the runway at Bedford, and they had sent me to the smallest aircraft-carrier in the world! The CO, Lyn Middleton, gave me my deck-landing brief in Ronnie's Bar at Halfar. This was the shortest and most succinct brief of my whole flying career. He cleared the locals off the dartboard, drew a deck and the circuit pattern and in the next two

> minutes told me how to deck land a Buccaneer. 'Any questions?' he asked as I was backed up against the wall with his nose about two inches from mine. He must have thought that I understood the brief because he then said that if I did what he had briefed, my first deck landing would be my best and my third, if I survived it, would be my worst. I stuck to his brief and his predictions were absolutely correct. I survived the third but only after having gouged a chunk out of the round-down [stern of the ship] with the hook. Commander Air grabbed me by the collar, marched me down the deck and showed me the error of my ways. How easily over-confidence can creep in after just two sorties. I finished my tour, two years later, with 600 hours of superb flying with the Fleet Air Arm, having dropped or fired more weapons than in any comparable time in the RAF.

Events overseas were keeping the embarked squadrons busy. The run-down to final withdrawal from Aden created a need to reinforce the RAF squadrons that were steadily being withdrawn, and the outbound HMS *Hermes* met up with the homecoming HMS *Victorious*. Together with the Sea Vixens of both carrier air groups and twenty-seven Khormaksar-based Hunters, a very powerful show of force of fifty-five aircraft impressed the local Aden dignitaries. Later in the year, 800 Squadron, embarked in HMS *Eagle*, covered the final withdrawal of British forces from Aden. With the withdrawal of the RAF's 1417 Flight of Hunters, the Buccaneers carried out a number of photographic reconnaissance sorties to locate forces of the South Yemen Army. On the day of withdrawal, 29 November 1967, the Squadron maintained a continuous airborne alert of two aircraft armed with rockets, with two further aircraft remaining on deck alert armed with eight 1,000-lb bombs each. The last reconnaissance sorties were flown and the squadron diarist

Three Buccaneer S 2 aircraft of 809 Squadron practise over Lossiemouth for the 1968 Farnborough Air Show. The all dark-sea grey scheme was introduced at this time and the Squadron's phoenix badge is prominent on the fin. (*Norman Roberson*)

recorded: 'The Squadron flew the last two British military aircraft that will be seen up-country in the Federation for some time to come.'

The crucial role played by carrier-borne air power was not lost on those critics who had vehemently opposed the recent decision to scrap the Navy's aircraft-carriers. Finally, Flight Lieutenant Tim Cockerell took off from HMS *Eagle* on the long trip to Bahrain with film for the BBC recording the final moments of the 128 years of British rule in the Federation. As he pointed out, 'It was the days before satellites.' So ended another chapter in the steady British withdrawal from east of Suez.

Exercise 'Bobbin Plus' was planned to demonstrate the ability of the Royal Navy to reinforce an aircraft-carrier in the Far East with additional aircraft. Four aircraft were to leave Lossiemouth in two pairs to land on HMS *Hermes* operating off the west coast of Malaysia. The task was allocated to 803 Squadron, which had formed as the Buccaneer trials squadron a year earlier. The four participating crews, led by the CO, Lieutenant-Commander 'Hoddy' Hoddinott, spent the week prior to departure practising air-to-air refuelling with the RAF's Victor tankers, which would accompany the Buccaneers. This training phase culminated in a five-hour cross-country with the tankers.

The first two aircraft departed on 19 August 1968, arriving in Nicosia five hours later after twice air-to-air refuelling from the Victors. The following day they departed for the island of Masirah, as the second pair took off from Lossiemouth. The pilots of the second pair were the CO and Lieutenant-Commander Jeremy Nichols, and they had for their observers Lieutenant Steve Lazenby and Admiral Sir

809 Squadron aircraft tensioned for launch from HMS *Hermes*, with a second about to have the strop fixed before the shuttle moves forward to tension the aircraft in to the nose-up attitude. The larger air intakes for the Rolls Royce Spey engine show prominently. (*Norman Roberson*)

Michael Le Fanu. The presence of the First Sea Lord in the back of XV 152 was a closely guarded secret. He had arrived at Lossiemouth in a Buccaneer the day before to complete his preparations and briefings. The four Buccaneers joined up at Masirah before setting off with their three Victor tankers for Gan, which was reached safely on 22 August despite numerous tropical thunderstorms in the area. The following day two pairs, with their Victor tankers, took off at ten-minute intervals and joined up at the top of the climb and set heading between the Nicobar Islands and Indonesia before turning towards Penang. Once in radio contact with HMS *Hermes* the tankers departed for RAAF Butterworth. Lieutenant-Commander 'Hoddy' Hoddinott takes up the final part of the story:

> After four relatively uneventful legs, all four Buccaneers landed on *Hermes* about 40 miles west of Butterworth during the morning of 23 August, after a flying time of eighteen hours. The First Sea Lord's objective had been to make a 'flying' visit to *Hermes* and he had been making like a Buccaneer observer since the early morning take-off from

HMS *Hermes* is steaming at speed ready to 'land on' its aircraft, but not before Lieutenant Robin Cox and Flight Lieutenant Norman Roberson and their leader make a low, fast pass down the port side. (*Norman Roberson*)

Lossiemouth. After a glass of champagne and lunch in the Wardroom, and with the main aim of the exercise completed, the Buccaneers were catapulted off the carrier before heading to RAF Changi, leaving the Admiral on the carrier's bridge finishing off the champagne.

The return route on 28 August differed only in using RAF Muharraq instead of Masirah but the same routine applied, a 5.15 a.m. take off, flying one leg each day, before reaching Lossiemouth at midday on 1 September after a six-hour flight from Nicosia, giving a total time of just under thirty-seven hours for the round trip.

All in all, not a bad run ashore!!

The very nature of aircraft-carrier operations required the aircrews to be proficient in many roles, and, as frequently happened, they often had to react to different scenarios at short notice. The Buccaneer was very much a multi-role strike and attack aircraft capable of delivering bombs and rockets, by day and night, from various attack modes in the anti-shipping, counter-air, interdiction and close support roles. In addition, the aircraft regularly carried out visual and photographic reconnaissance and there was usually one aircraft in the air-to-air refuelling fit. During periods at sea all these roles were practised using nearby shore-based targets or against friendly warships, many of them towing a 'splash' target. Practice and live weapons were released on almost every sortie, many of which included air-to-air refuelling. The splash target was a simple wooden frame with metal scoops, towed some 400 yards behind the carrier or one of the escort ships, and most sorties concluded with bombing or rocket attacks against the target. This provided great entertainment for the sailors on board the ships and sometimes a few anxious moments for the Captain. Peter Sturt remembers one such incident:

> Bombing the splash had its amusing moments, especially when we tried to persuade the Captain that we wanted to toss bombs at the splash target by locking on with our radars to the carrier and feeding an offset into the weapon system computer to give us a hit on the towed target. It took two months to convince him that we were not totally mad and that we would guarantee that it was impossible to hit the ship because we would be pointing aft of 'his' ship on the low-level approach before pulling up to release the bombs. It took another month of successful attacks with practice bombs before he reluctantly let us loose with some inert 1,000-lb bombs. For some unaccountable reason he baulked when we suggested using HE [High Explosive]!

An 809 Squadron aircraft is tensioned on the starboard catapult of HMS *Hermes* just prior to launch. There is very little clearance on the starboard side. (*Norman Roberson*)

Typical of the regular exercises carried out by an embarked Buccaneer squadron was Exercise 'Shadow' conducted off the east coast of Australia. The aim of the exercise was for HMS *Hermes* and escorts to ensure the safe passage of an Amphibious Assault Group headed by HMS *Bulwark* from the Bismarck Sea to a landing area in Queensland. Opposing this task force were ships and submarines of the Royal Australian and Royal New Zealand Navies and land-based aircraft of the Royal Australian Air Force and Navy. The track of the Task Force was planned to ensure a surface encounter and to give the submarines maximum opportunity for interceptions.

The exercise commenced in the early hours of 29 September 1968 when a Buccaneer of 801 Squadron took off for a shipping probe looking for fast patrol boats (FPB) along the coast of New Guinea. Contact was made, two Buccaneers were launched to carry out an attack and a practice bomb was dropped 200 yards ahead of one of the FPBs. This caused some consternation since the briefing should have said, 'not closer than 2,000 yards ahead'! Two further strikes during the morning effectively eliminated the FPB threat but numerous long-range searches failed to locate an 'enemy' Surface Action Group (SAG) threatening the Task Force. In the following period the FPBs were 'resurrected' and searches were conducted in poor weather. By the fourth day the Task Force was within striking range of the enemy coast and two strikes were launched against lines of communication. Six aircraft were launched for the first strike and transited at high level before letting down to low level to attack two bridges. Later in the day a further strike was carried out, with the Buccaneer tanker playing an important role.

As the Task Force approached the landing area, the Buccaneers found themselves seeking out and attacking more FPBs, this time using rockets fired in a 10° dive. Once the area had been cleared of this potent threat, the amphibious landing phase commenced, with the Buccaneers tasked with Close Air Support (CAS). Twelve sorties were flown against targets grouped around the landing area, with others in the area of an impending airborne assault. The targets were invariably mortar or gun positions that were difficult to locate until they fired. In the meantime, a single Buccaneer was launched in the photographic reconnaissance fit to take photographs and report on a river bed to assess its suitability as a hovercraft landing area.

The next phase saw the Squadron carrying out live FAC on Townshend Island range. The squadron diarist recorded the events of the day:

> The first five sorties carried 1,000-lb bombs, both impact and VT fused, and others had two full pods of rockets, one live and one inert. For most pilots it was the first occasion to fire full pods of rockets and the quantity of smoke and the noise took them by surprise. A third attack to clear both pods was flown past the range hut! Further sorties carried 1,000-lb bombs and these were dropped in various dive-bombing modes. All marking was visual by an airborne FAC who appeared to err on the generous side – probably as they had never seen 1,000-lb bombs explode at such close range before. It was a good day's flying in which the squadron armourers did a great job and the aircrew enjoyed the opportunity to drop so many live weapons.

After a day of flying armed reconnaissance sorties, the Task Force had moved further south to strike the RAAF airfield at Williamstown. Two aircraft were launched on a long-range (600 miles) photographic reconnaissance mission to the airfield. After air-to-air refuelling they let down to low level, evaded the fighter patrols and returned at high level with some excellent photographs that formed the basis for the following day's attacks. At first light on the following day, four aircraft launched for a high-level transit to attack the airfield. Once low level the formation split into two sections for a coordinated attack, which was completely successful. In the meantime, Sea Vixens had located the enemy SAG and three Buccaneers carried out a successful attack, including dropping practice bombs on a splash target towed by the obliging enemy.

On the final day further attacks were mounted against Williamstown airfield. The Buccaneers were able to transit at low level all the way and they had a Sea Vixen fighter escort to take care of the opposing Mirage fighters. Two four-ship attacks had been made by midday when the ten-day exercise finished. 801 Squadron had flown 120 out of 132 tasked sorties, accumulating 187 hours. On three occasions all the squadron aircraft were airborne at the same time, with constant role changes placing tremendous demands on the maintenance ratings. The tanker aircraft was in constant demand and on one occasion was turned round and airborne just 30 minutes after hooking on from the previous sortie.

The exercise has been described in some detail to highlight the great variety of roles fulfilled by an embarked Buccaneer squadron. At the end of every sortie, of course, was the not unimportant task of finding the carrier and landing back on board safely, often with the deck pitching and frequently without a diversion airfield. Add some night-flying under similar conditions and life became interesting – some might say exciting. It was certainly exhilarating and challenging flying. Inevitably, a number of aircraft were lost in accidents that were due entirely to the nature of deck landings. Most would have landed with complete safety had they been operating from runways. In the early days, a Mark 1 of 800 Squadron was attempting to land on HMS *Eagle* but missed the wires, and as the pilot applied full power, the port engine failed so the aircraft was unable to climb away and the crew ejected safely at a perilously low

After the demise of the Scimitar tankers, each squadron maintained one aircraft in the air-to-air refuelling fit. The FRL Mark 20 refuelling pod was always carried on the starboard inner pylon. The ram air turbine on the front generated all the power necessary to operate the refuelling equipment, which the observer operated from a panel on the port side of his cockpit. (*P.H.T. Green*)

height. Had they been landing at an airfield, the aircraft would have simply touched down a few yards further down the runway. Perhaps the most bizarre loss occurred towards the end of 801 Squadron's final commission on HMS *Hermes*. Lieutenant 'Pony' Moore was the pilot of XV 167 and recalls the incident:

> My observer, Mike Cunningham, and I were tasked to fly a long-range probe sortie from *Hermes* and we were to be launched first, immediately before the Gannets, which was not the normal practice. We taxied forward to the port catapult and the flight-deck crew attached the hold-back to the deck, secured the strop and then the aircraft was tensioned. We completed our pre-launch checks and I had just signalled the 'OK' to the Flight Deck Officer when the nose of the aircraft dropped to the deck with a thump and we started moving forward. I thought we had got a cold shot [insufficient steam pressure to give the catapult enough inertia]. Flyco started shouting 'Brakes, brakes' over the R/T but I realised we were not going to stop and called 'Eject, eject'. Mike went instantly. I looked in the mirror and saw that he had gone and, just as the nose-wheel was going over the front of the bow, I ejected. Thankfully, the aircraft had just been modified with the rocket ejector seat. Within seconds I separated from the seat and my parachute snagged on one of the radio aerials on the starboard side but it ripped and I fell in to the sea. In the meantime, Mike looked as if he would land on the deck and the Gannets, waiting to launch, were all feathering their propellers. In fact, he just missed the stern and landed in the wake. Hermes was doing 22 knots and churning up a great wake and she was towing a splash target. An Able Seaman had the presence of mind to hack the cable and within seconds Mike was being winched into the SAR helicopter. By now the Captain had gone from full ahead to full astern and I was then picked up and was in bed in sick quarters three minutes after I pulled the ejection seat handle.

This was the first ejection using the new rocket seat from an almost stationary aircraft, and there is no doubt that the crew would not have survived the accident had the old 90-kts seats still been fitted. The subsequent investigation discovered that the holdback had been kinked when fitted, and as the pilot applied full power, the surge straightened it and the weak link sheared before the catapult had been fired. This was 'Pony' Moore's second ejection. During his training the undercarriage of his Buccaneer failed to lower and he was ordered to climb to 9,000 ft and eject into the sea just off the beach at Lossiemouth.

The anti-aircraft defences of Soviet warships improved rapidly during the 1960s, yet the high-performance Buccaneer still had no realistic stand-off weapon. The Martin-Marietta Bullpup A missile had been procured in the early 1960s for the Buccaneer and was the first attempt to provide a stand-off weapon delivery capability. The missile was built around a standard 250-lb bomb warhead and featured four small delta-control wings at the front and four larger aft wings. A solid-fuelled rocket motor provided a range of about five miles. Guidance was by radio command from inputs made by the pilot, who centred his sight on the target before launch. Flares in the rear of the missile allowed him to follow it visually after launch and send mid-course control corrections as necessary. After initial trials, the missile was fired occasionally, but in November 1969, 809 Squadron carried out some novel trials in an attempt to make greater use of the missile's limited stand-off capability.

The aim was to discover a mode of delivering the missile against ships in a less suicidal way than in a steady dive, which was the original tactic. After countless practice runs on the 'Bullpup Trainer,' which resembled a cheap fairground game machine, crews were selected to participate in the trial. The live attacks were flown against the small rocky outcrop of Gralis Sgier located in inhospitable seas well to the north-west of Cape Wrath. Two aircraft approached the target at high speed and at a pre-determined range the 'controlling aircraft' reduced speed to 200 kts whilst the firing aircraft sped ahead to the missile release range and fired the missile in a nose-up

An 809 Squadron Buccaneer about to catch number two wire (number one is not fitted). With two aircraft lashed down in Fly Four, the pilot needs to be lined up perfectly. The aircraft was flown straight onto the deck without any flare, and as it touched the deck, the pilot applied full power and closed the airbrake ready for a 'bolter' and another attempt. The ship is towing a splash target seen clearly in the ship's wake. (*Norman Roberson*)

attitude to give it a ballistic trajectory. After the release the firing aircraft escaped with a tight turn away. The ballistic trajectory was necessary to help overcome the considerable gravity drop during the long time of flight of the missile. Meanwhile the pilot in the 'controlling aircraft' a few miles behind kept the flare on the missile lined up with the target. The trials were only partially successful, and, although the aircraft were less vulnerable than with the earlier method, the tactics were inflexible and used two aircraft to achieve very modest results. With the anticipated introduction of Martel (Missile Anti-Radar TELevision), the next-generation missile, the Bullpup did not figure prominently in the attack profiles of the Buccaneer. Lieutenant-Commander Frank Cox was the Squadron Air Warfare Instructor (AWI) tasked with co-ordinating the trial, and he remembers two incidents that highlighted the unexpected when carrying out trials:

> The first occurred when I was leading three aircraft to fire four missiles between us. We let down through broken cloud in the range area and set ourselves up for the first attack. The approach went well and the missile was fired at the optimum range.

We were all taken aback when, two seconds later, the missile decided to emulate a Saturn moon rocket and it disappeared vertically into the overcast. Not surprisingly this caused some consternation amongst the watching crews who wondered where and when the errant missile would re-appear.

The second incident occurred towards the end of the trial. Brian Jackson-Dooley was my observer and we started the take-off roll down Lossiemouth's runway 23, with full fuel and two live missiles, into murky weather and a 200-ft cloud base. As the aircraft rotated, the starboard engine decided to quit in spectacular fashion, with a huge explosion accompanied by flames leaping out of the intake and an enquiring expletive from the back seat. I assured Brian that the single-engine performance was proving adequate to propel the entire mass into the air and to climb clear of the (now unseen) high ground. We settled back to climb to a safe height, dumped fuel and returned for an uneventful landing. The end of another day at the office!

By the beginning of 1970 the run-down of the fixed-wing carrier force had gathered momentum. Following a disastrous fire in 1967, HMS *Victorious* had been taken out of service and was waiting to be scrapped, and two years later, a decision was taken to decommission HMS *Eagle*, and the front-line Buccaneer squadrons started to decommission. At the Lossiemouth Air Day in July 1970, 801 Squadron flew over in formation and the squadron diary records: 'Our formation was a fitting finale to the Air Day flying programme but also to our own squadron flying. This was the last full day for 801 as a front-line Naval Air Squadron and we slip into history.'

Meanwhile, 800 Squadron was completing its final cruise in the Far East, and in January 1972, HMS *Eagle* sailed into Portsmouth for the last time after thirty years of service. Ten aircraft had flown off the carrier a few days earlier and were preparing to fly over the ship as it entered harbour. Ironically, and sadly, the weather was totally unsuitable for flying. The great ship did not receive the salute she deserved and 800 Squadron was denied its final sortie before disbanding. The Squadron Commander captured the feeling of his men: 'In this matter-of-fact and typically naval fashion, thirty-nine years of aviation history were wrapped up and disposed of, following a decision taken purely on political and economic grounds.'

The steady run-down of the Buccaneer squadrons left 809 Squadron embarked in HMS *Ark Royal*, the last remaining fixed-wing carrier, as the only Fleet Air Arm strike-attack squadron after the decommissioning of 800 Squadron. Ironically, the flexibility of carrier-borne aircraft and the very long range of the Buccaneer were amply demonstrated in January 1972. Tension had increased between British Honduras (later to gain independence as Belize) and Guatemala. HMS *Ark Royal* was ordered to steam towards Honduras and provide an 'air presence' over the colony as soon as possible. On 29 January 1972, when the ship was 1,200 miles away, two Buccaneers were launched, together with two Buccaneer tankers. After transferring fuel 400 miles from the carrier, the two tankers returned as the pair of probe aircraft carried on to Belize City and made their presence known before heading back. The two tankers had refuelled and been relaunched to make a rendezvous with the returning Buccaneers that finally landed back on HMS *Ark Royal* after a six-hour sortie. After participating in exercises on the eastern USA seaboard and in the North Atlantic, 809 Squadron disembarked to RAF Honington in Suffolk following the transfer of RNAS Lossiemouth to the Royal Air Force. Seven aircraft led by the Commanding Officer, Lieutenant-Commander Fred de la Billière, landed at Honington on 18 October 1972, where the Squadron 'received a royal welcome from the people at Honington and the local press'. The Suffolk airfield remained the shore base of the Squadron until it was decommissioned in November 1978.

CHAPTER 4

Into Royal Air Force Service

As early as 1957, a version of the Buccaneer had been offered to the Royal Air Force as a Canberra replacement, but the supersonic TSR 2 had been chosen to fulfil Air Staff Requirement 339, and the NA 39, as the Buccaneer was then known, was not considered further. However, following a Defence Review initiated by the Labour Government in 1964, there were two policy decisions that changed the whole structure of the RAF's future strike aircraft programme, and this, in turn, determined the long-term future of the Buccaneer.

First was the cancellation of the TSR 2 programme in April 1965. The Brough firm, now part of the Hawker Siddeley Group, offered an advanced Buccaneer Mark 2 as a replacement for the TSR 2, but the Government decided to place an order for fifty General Dynamics F-111K instead. Secondly, in February 1966, it was

Following the decision to transfer Buccaneers from the Royal Navy to the RAF, XV 350 was the first aircraft to be modified to meet RAF requirements. The aircraft spent almost the whole of its life on the strength of the A&AEE at Boscombe Down, where it carried out trials work. Here it is armed with anti-radar Martel missiles. (*Author's Collection*)

announced that CVA 01, the Royal Navy's follow-on fixed-wing aircraft-carrier programme, had also been cancelled. Within eighteen months, the F-111 order was cancelled due to escalating costs and it was announced that the F-4 Phantom would be purchased for RAF attack operations, with twenty-six Buccaneer S 2Bs ordered for the strike role. This was soon followed by an order for seventeen additional aircraft, together with an announcement that the RAF would receive sixty-four Royal Navy Buccaneers as the carriers were phased out of service. It was also announced that the RAF would gradually assume the responsibility for strike/attack operations in support of maritime operations, as the carriers were withdrawn.

To avoid delays in the delivery of the new-build Mark 2B aircraft it was decided to manufacture them with most of the 'navalised' features such as wing-fold and the hook. However, the aircraft had a higher all-up weight, strengthened undercarriage and a modified wing that would enable the carriage of the Martel missile due to enter service in the early 1970s. The most innovative modification was to fit a conformal 425-gallon fuel tank into the outer skin of the bomb bay door. There was virtually no extra drag penalty and the already impressive range of the aircraft was extended even further.

The first Buccaneer converted to RAF requirements was XV 350, which made its maiden flight in modified form on 11 February 1969. It was allocated to Boscombe Down for flight trials and it continued with this valuable work for the majority of its existence. It was joined by the first production Mark S2B, XW 525, fitted with the new bomb door fuel tank.

Small numbers of RAF aircrew had been seconded to the Royal Navy Buccaneer squadrons since 1965. The announcement that the aircraft-carriers would be phased out affected the recruitment of Royal Navy pilots and observers and there was an increasing requirement for the RAF to provide additional crews. By 1969 some thirty 'light blue' pilots and navigators were flying on naval squadrons. Needless to say, the majority would not be available to return to RAF service for two or three years, so there was a significant requirement to train crews for the new RAF squadrons, due to start forming in late 1969.

The delays caused by the cancellation of various strike/attack aircraft projects had created an urgent need to get the Buccaneer into RAF service quickly. Since the Royal Navy already had an operational training organisation in existence it was decided to form the first two RAF squadrons before forming an Operational Conversion Unit (OCU), and to use 736 Squadron's training facilities for the first eight RAF courses, each consisting of four crews. The Navy establishment of aircraft and personnel for 736 Squadron was based on the need to train a relatively small number of crews for the Fleet Air Arm squadrons, so additional resources had to be found to cope with this new training task.

Six RAF aircrew flying with Navy squadrons were transferred to 736 Squadron as instructors. The plan was for the RAF courses to be flown entirely on the Buccaneer S 1, with the exception of three familiarisation sorties on the Mark 2 at the end of the course. Six Mark 1 aircraft were brought out of long-term storage and reactivated, and an engineer officer, Flight Lieutenant John Harvey, and fifty RAF technicians were posted in to help maintain these aircraft and to learn engineering skills for subsequent use on the RAF's Buccaneer squadrons.

The first RAF long course began at Lossiemouth on 19 May 1969, with new courses starting at three-monthly intervals. Crews on these courses were destined to form the RAF's first two Buccaneer squadrons, and the two-year programme ran very successfully. The excitement of a posting to the Buccaneer is well captured by Flying Officer Al Beaton, one of the first RAF pilots to join the force direct from training:

> The Graduation speech and postings announced at the Dining-In Night in August 1968 for No. 40 Course at RAF Valley was not just the ultimate in a sense of relief at having passed a gruelling flying course, it was an unbelievable moment in life when a dream comes true. Then the postings were announced with Lightnings, Hunters, Canberras and even CFS postings allocated first, but the best had been saved till last; Bill Cope and I were the first two RAF first tourists being posted to the Buccaneer. The RAF's exciting new low-level combat aircraft was entering service and we had just timed it perfectly. We were the centres of congratulations with a fair measure of envy; I just remember feeling so incredibly lucky. I had always wanted to fly two-seat low level, TSR 2 had been my inspiration, but the Buccaneer soon took on that driving force that ambition brings. High speed, low level, close to the ground or over the sea, the exhilaration and total sense of freedom that low level brings and no other role can provide. How lucky I was.

Flight Lieutenant Tom Eeles, who had recently completed an embarked tour with 801 Squadron, was the RAF flying instructor on 736 Squadron at the time and he regularly found himself in the back seat, talking pilots through their first familiarisation sortie. On 1 December 1970, first-tour pilot Flying Officer Ivor Evans was briefed for his first Buccaneer sortie. Tom Eeles was programmed to be the 'talking ballast' in the back seat of XN 951 and he relates the event:

> By the time Ivor's course arrived at Lossiemouth the Mark 1s were getting decidedly tired. Their Gyron Junior engines, never known for their user-friendly handling characteristics, caused us numerous problems. On Ivor's 'Fam One' we had great difficulty getting the port engine to accelerate through the IGV range before take-off but, with

To meet the unexpected requirement to train over thirty crews for the first RAF squadrons, a number of Mark 1 aircraft were brought out of storage and serviced by RAF ground crews attached to 736 Squadron at RNAS Lossiemouth. This aircraft, XN 965, is fitted with practice bomb carriers, each capable of carrying two 25-lb practice bombs. (*P.H.T. Green*)

persistence, it finally wound up and off we went. All went well until we returned to the circuit. We ended up too high and close on the first circuit and at 200 ft I told Ivor to overshoot. He put on full power but all that happened in the port engine was a great wheezing and banging noise, but no thrust. With commendable alacrity for a pilot on his first sortie, Ivor got the wheels up and the airbrake in but with flap down and blow selected, the only influence on our progress with one gutless Gyron Junior was Isaac Newton's first law. It rapidly became evident that the only way in which the sortie could be concluded satisfactorily was through the use of Martin Baker's rocket-assisted deckchair. Shouting 'eject, eject' I pulled the bottom handle and there was an almighty bang and within seconds I had landed in an untidy heap.

After thanking the Almighty and thinking that my back hurt, I thought I must quickly erect my SARBE beacon in order to qualify for a very nice silver tankard handed out to genuine users by the makers of the product. At this point an asbestos-suited fireman appeared on the scene and I told him to push off as I still hadn't erected the aerial. Given that I was lying in the middle of Lossiemouth airfield in front of the control tower, he clearly thought I was delirious and had taken leave of my senses so restrained me from taking any further action. Ivor also jumped out successfully and the hapless Buccaneer flopped onto the airfield with the starboard engine still running at full power until the fire crews filled it with foam. This action generated clouds of noxious fumes, which drifted downwind into the Wardroom bar and disturbed the lunch-time drinkers!

Exactly one week later, Flying Officer Pete Warren and his navigator, Pilot Officer Peter Paines, took off in XN 968 on their fourth Buccaneer sortie and their first together as a crew. Just after take-off and climbing through 1,500 ft, there was a catastrophic uncontained engine failure in the starboard engine. Both crew ejected, but the navigator's seat was damaged as it shattered the canopy and, with insufficient height, his attempted manual separation from the seat failed and he was killed.

The subsequent investigation revealed serious fatigue problems in the turbine of the Gyron Junior engine, which it was not considered economical to rectify. This signalled the end of the Buccaneer S 1 and, apart from some test and delivery flights, the aircraft did not fly again. The four crews on the last 736 Squadron-trained RAF course converted to the Mark 2 and completed their training in May 1971. The Squadron continued to operate until early 1972, when it was descommissioned and all Buccaneer training was transferred to the newly formed 237 OCU based at Honington.

Royal Air Force Honington in mid-Suffolk had been selected as the home for the F-111 force, and work had commenced to prepare the station to receive and support the aircraft. With the cancellation of the aircraft, it was decided that the RAF's UK-based Buccaneer force would occupy the station, and the first unit to arrive was the re-formed 12 Squadron, a famous bomber unit number. Shortly after lunch on 1 October 1969 four Buccaneers, led by the Squadron Commander, Wing Commander Geoff Davies AFC, broke into the Honington circuit, landed on the newly resurfaced runway and taxied in to a champagne welcome. Few of those present could have anticipated that the Buccaneer would serve for a further twenty-five years in RAF service. The Squadron was equipped with modified ex-Fleet Air Arm Mark 2s and was assigned to SACLANT (Supreme Allied Commander Atlantic) in the maritime strike/attack role under the operational control of Headquarters No. 1 (Bomber) Group. There were many who felt that the Squadron should have formed part of No. 18 (Maritime) Group; twelve years later the Buccaneer Maritime Wing was finally transferred to 18 Group.

Exactly one year after 12 Squadron's arrival at Honington, another famous bomber unit was re-formed, and XV Squadron became the second RAF Buccaneer squadron. Under the command of Wing Commander David Collins, XV Squadron

No. 12 Squadron formed as the first RAF Buccaneer squadron on 1 October 1969 when four ex-Royal Navy S. 2As arrived at RAF Honington. The first 12 Squadron crews led by the Squadron Commander, Wing Commander Geoff Davies, flying XV 347, flew the aircraft. The aircraft were finished in gloss dark green and dark sea grey upper surfaces and light grey undersides, and the earlier A-type national markings. (*MOD/Crown Copyright*)

received the first new-build S Mark 2B aircraft, and the crews spent the first four months working-up at Honington before moving to their permanent base at RAF Laarbruch on the Dutch-German border. The Squadron was assigned to SACEUR (Supreme Allied Commander Europe) in the strike/attack role and came under the operational control of Headquarters Second Allied Tactical Air Force. In October 1972, 16 Squadron, commanded by Wing Commander 'Bodger' Edwards, formed at Laarbruch as the second RAF Germany-based SACEUR-assigned squadron. On 1 July 1974, 208 Squadron, commanded by Wing Commander Peter Rogers, formed at Honington with Buccaneer S 2A aircraft to operate in the overland role and assigned to SACEUR for operations in the AFNORTH region.

CHAPTER 5

Training

As XV Squadron departed for Germany, 237 Operational Conversion Unit (OCU) formed at Honington on 1 March 1971 under the command of Wing Commander Tony Fraser and equipped with ex-Royal Navy Buccaneer S 2 aircraft. The RAF instructor crews serving with 736 Squadron were transferred to the OCU and were soon joined by other RAF crews on completion of their exchange tours with the Royal Navy and by experienced crews from 12 Squadron. Flight Lieutenant John Harvey and his ground tradesman, serving with 736 Squadron at Lossiemouth, also moved to Honington. Three months after forming, the OCU assumed responsibility for the training of all future RAF Buccaneer crews, and the first Long Course, No. 9 Course, commenced training. With the decommissioning of 736 Squadron twelve months later, the OCU assumed the additional

The first Buccaneer assigned to 237 OCU was XT 287, an ex-Royal Navy S. 2A, seen here fitted with wing tanks and a 2-in rocket pod. The unit badge, a mortar board crossed with a pair of cutlasses, is on the port engine cowling. (*MAP*)

responsibility of training all future Navy Buccaneer aircrew. Two experienced Royal Navy Buccaneer crews joined the instructional staff of 237 OCU, and the mix of dark and light blue instructors continued to be a feature for the next few years until 809, the last of the Royal Navy squadrons, was decommissioned. As Tom Eeles remarked: 'The close integration of RAF and RN aircrew during their operational flying training on the Buccaneer that had started in 1965 explains why there has always been a very strong bond of friendship between dark and light blue Buccaneer aircrew.'

This bond was soon extended to the United States Air Force and Navy, with the arrival of the first combat-experienced crews serving as part of an exchange scheme. For the next twenty years there was always a USAF instructor crew serving on the OCU and others served on the operational maritime squadrons.

The initial task of the OCU was to train the crews who formed XV and 16 Squadron and to train replacement crews for 12 and 809 Squadrons. The conversion syllabus was very similar to that used on 736 Squadron, but certain changes were made to meet the RAF's overland requirements. It also had to take account of a different weather factor in East Anglia. The Chief Flying Instructor, Squadron Leader David Mulinder observed:

> The favourable weather factor enjoyed at Lossiemouth, allied to two superb and very adjacent bombing ranges [Tain and Rosehearty], for which there was little competition, conferred a great advantage on those trained in Morayshire and provided the instructors on 237 OCU with a subject of unending fascination as we stared gloomily at the fog, mist, low stratus, rain and poor visibility with which many of our days started . . . and finished.

In preparing crews for the front-line squadrons, background and experience played an important part. Second-tourist crews destined for RAF squadrons flew approximately fifty-five hours in the Buccaneer and first tourist crews were given an extra ten hours. Most Navy crews were experienced on the aircraft and completed a thirty-hour refresher course. During the early 1970s, an increasing number of RAF first-tourists were sent to 809 Squadron, and on completion of the long course, they continued with a pre-embarkation course of thirty-six hours. This latter phase covered all the naval-orientated sorties such as catapult launches, deck-landing practice and maritime tactics.

Each main course began with two weeks' ground school, followed by ten days in the simulator. The Mark 2 simulators at Honington were very much more capable than the original Mark 1 simulator at Lossiemouth and provided an excellent introduction to the aircraft. During this phase the student pilots flew four sorties in the Hunter T 8b carrying out airborne training with the IFIS, as fitted in the Buccaneer. It was then time to fly the Buccaneer.

The aircraft had outstanding handling qualities at high speed and low level, but it was a different situation once speed was reduced below 300 knots and the landing configuration was selected. Approaches in different configurations were practised in the simulator, where great emphasis

Crews destined for the embarked Royal Navy squadrons visited RAE Bedford to experience a catapult launch. A 237 OCU aircraft is tensioned on the Static Steam Catapult ready to be launched. Judging by the red flag, there is a reasonable head wind component, but this was not always the case. (*Tom Eeles*)

was placed on completing the checks correctly and flying accurately.

To reduce the landing speed, a 'blown' approach was the standard recovery. This was flown at a steady attitude and power, with the angle of attack constant. The airflow direction detector (ADD) gave a visual and audio indication of the angle of attack, with a 'steady' note indicating that the speed was within a knot of the datum speed. High speed was indicated by a high frequency 'bleep' and low speed by a lower frequency of 'bloops', with a small band where the steady note was overlaid by appropriate bleeps or bloops. The autostabilisers were selected to 'approach' to provide greater control and stability, and the aileron gear change was set to 'low speed', giving increased roll control in the approach configurations. Flaps, aileron droop and tailplane flap were always selected in stages, with each monitored to check that all three, in particular aileron droop and tailplane flap, moved and stopped together. If the aileron droop became desynchronised by more than one step, pitch control could be lost, and this once had fatal results. Without 'blow', the maximum safe configuration was 45-10-10 (wing flap, aileron droop, tailplane flap) resulting in a datum speed of 17 knots faster than the blown approach speed using 45-25-25. The configuration 30-20-20 was used for blown take-offs or single-engine blown approaches. As

The two-seat Hunter T 7/8s were an integral part of the Buccaneer force. They were equipped with the Buccaneer instrument panel in the left-hand seat and, with no dual-control Buccaneer, they were used extensively for routine pilot instrument ratings and regular check sorties. The later OCU markings are in evidence and the Buccaneers carry the station codes with the *C representing 'cutlass' for the OCU. (*BAe Systems*)

The pilot's cockpit, dominated by the Integrated Flight Instrument System (IFIS) in the centre. Above the altitude indicator is a strip airspeed indicator calibrated in knots and Mach number. The strike sight is in the folded position, and to the left, is the very accurate deck-landing airspeed indicator. The engine instruments and the blow gauges on the starboard side could be clearly seen and monitored by the observer/navigator. (*BAe Systems*)

Bruce Chapple commented, '45-25-25 unblown was not good for long life and good health'.

On a first solo flight, all these configurations were practiced at medium level before the exercise concentrated on setting up the aircraft for a practice, straight-in, blown approach on datum at 45-25-25, ensuring a steady pitch attitude and power to maintain a 700-ft rate of descent. Once completed, it was time to return to the circuit and carry out a series of approaches. The Buccaneer was flown at a continuous rate of descent, without an attempt to flare before touchdown, until the ground intervened, when full power was selected as the airbrake was closed for a roller landing.

The progression from the simulator to Hunter to Buccaneer stood the test of time, and the vast majority of first solos passed without incident. However, as Bill Ryce described in Chapter Two, instructors flying on Fam 1 sorties sometimes had to deal with some interesting problems on this first sortie. Captain Ken Alley was a USAF pilot instructor on exchange to 237 OCU, and recalls (in his Tennessee English!) sitting in the back for Flying Officer Keith Hildred's first sortie in a Buccaneer:

> During my instructor training I was given a back seat check out with the uncomfortable realization of no stick, throttles, rudder or attitude indicator. I had soloed several students when I was doing a Fam 1 with Keith Hildred. He was doing OK but we were told to break off our first straight-in approach so we went to the overhead to join the visual circuit. About half way round the final turn, with full flaps, droop and blow, the Buccaneer got a little quieter. We had lost the right engine. I shouted the recovery procedures to Keith and he correctly applied them but it still looked like we were not going to make the go-round. I informed Tower of our engine loss and the expected ejection. By the time everything was cleaned up we could just maintain altitude and airspeed and crossed the hangars [at right angles to the runway] with a few feet to spare. This poor student had not even performed a circuit or roller in the Buccaneer and now he had to land it from a single-engine approach. I told him to just worry about getting it down in the first half of the runway and the hook plus the arresting gear would do the rest. We successfully made it and stopped without the aid of the cable but there was a funny smell out of the front cockpit when we opened the canopy! After the debrief I was informed by the other instructors that they could not remember a successful single-engine recovery in the final turn in a fully blown configuration.

After a pilot's first solo, it was the job of the navigator to monitor and advise on pilot aircraft handling matters. Also, once a crew joined a squadron, the senior navigators were responsible for conducting the regular pilot 'operational checks'. In the early days, there was no formal training for navigator supervisors to assess handling skills, so a sortie was devised on the OCU during which a QFI demonstrated the various idiosyncrasies of the Buccaneer in the

A 12 Squadron aircraft turns finals in the 45-25-25 blown configuration with half airbrake selected. As the aircraft rolled out on finals full airbrake was selected. The tail skid is down and this prevented over-rotation during aerodynamic braking. (*MOD/Crown Copyright*)

'blown' configuration, the potential pitfalls and the warning signs of impending disaster. The demonstration was carried out at the end of a routine sortie, and was conducted at medium level before descending to the circuit. The medium-level portion dwelt on demonstrating, at a safe height, the effects of power, attitude and trim, particularly when incorrectly set and the situation was allowed to develop. Bruce Chapple developed the navigator's demonstration sortie and he describes the content:

> The aircraft was set up in the 45-25-25 approach configuration and the correct parameters were demonstrated before varying one parameter at a time, and examining the effect. The blow source was the HP compressor. The minimum blow pressure on the approach was twenty psi, which coincided with the HP rpm at 85 per cent. If power was reduced to this rpm and twenty psi with the ADD steady, the rate of descent increased to an interesting 4,000 ft per minute after a few seconds; the recovery took 800 ft! Another interesting phenomenon occurred if power was decreased abruptly. The decrease in boundary layer blow allowed the airflow to break away from the trailing edge, resulting in a very marked pitch up.
>
> An equally important factor in setting up an accurate approach was a steady, trimmed pitch attitude, without which a controlled approach could not be flown. This might be a statement of the obvious, but the culture shock of moving from the Hawk to the Hunter was enough to cause trepidation among some junior pilots, and the final move to a 20-ton beast with a mind of its own was, in some cases, enough to raise the laundry bill! There was also a side effect of the drooped ailerons, which increased adverse yaw. If bank was applied on the finals turn without the use of rudder, the aircraft barely turned at all, so a hefty boot of rudder to initiate the turn was essential.
>
> After the medium-level demonstration, an instrument approach was flown into the circuit,

> which reinforced the points shown earlier. This reflected the Fam (figure I) flown by the pilots, and provided a good background for the navigator supervisors and instructors who became very adept at critical and constructive analysis of their pilot's ability. It was their life insurance policy.

The more diverse roles of RAF squadrons demanded a greater concentration on night flying and overland tactics. Night flying was introduced when the students had some twenty-five hours' flying time on the Buccaneer. First the pilot had to gain a White Instrument Rating and fly a night check with a QFI in the Hunter, for this was a demanding phase. After two familiarisation flights and a low-level navigation sortie, the student crew graduated to night formation and bombing. This part of the course consumed fifteen hours and a high standard was demanded. After joining a squadron, a student crew would be expected to fly night formation for prolonged periods, attack targets under their own flares and indulge in the mystical art of 'basket dancing' with the Victor tanker. David Mulinder describes the final phase of the course:

> During the final sorties, both day and night, the student crews planned, briefed and flew live bombing attacks on various weapon ranges taking into account simulated intelligence, enemy defences, weather, terrain and types of attack. During the sortie they had to demonstrate their ability to find and describe targets, maintain station during formation dive-bombing attacks and evade a Hunter or Buccaneer 'bounce' flown by an instructor, while maintaining formation integrity before dropping accurate bombs. At the OCU we placed great emphasis on crew cooperation. The pace of Buccaneer operations was fast and the workload high. Aggressive thinking was actively encouraged, allied to good judgement and common sense, and a knowledge of each other's job so that the workload could be shared during the more critical phases.

This latter point was a fundamental feature of Buccaneer operations. Pilots and navigators had a detailed knowledge of each other's roles and this aspect received considerable emphasis on the OCU. It was continued on the squadrons and crews regularly flew 'reverse seat' sorties in the simulator to enhance their knowledge. The navigator monitored the pilot's actions throughout a sortie, and particularly in the circuit when the Buccaneer was always a handful for the pilot. Checks and vital actions were always based on 'challenge and response', and the navigator was able to visually monitor crucial actions such as the selection of flap and droop, blow pressures and fuel states. In a tactical situation at very low level, pilots had to concentrate on the terrain ahead, and it was often the case that the navigator would see a fighter threat first and he would control the tactics of the formation. Similarly, the pilot was able to monitor navigation and all pilots flew with a detailed target map, often flying the final stage of an attack unaided while the navigator monitored the radar threat warning receiver or made selections on the electronic countermeasures (ECM) active pod. Whenever possible, crews remained together and some outstanding partnerships were established.

The OCU was also responsible for certain post-graduate training for the squadrons. Weapons instructors were trained on a three-month course and instrument-rating examiners completed a course on the Hunter. The OCU was also responsible for an annual standardisation of all Buccaneer squadrons. To maintain their own currency and credibility, instructors regularly flew with the operational squadrons and participated fully in the frequent exercises. Another important task of the OCU was the Buccaneer Ground Servicing School through which the majority of RAF ground tradesmen had to pass before going to a squadron. A crucial factor in the life of every Buccaneer squadron and the OCU was the engineering organisation, and the Buccaneer force

Crew cooperation and teamwork were the hallmarks of the success of the Buccaneer force. The tandem cockpit provided outstanding lookout, and the observer/navigator's position higher and slightly offset allowed him to monitor many of the pilot's actions. The crew are sitting on rocket-assisted Type 6 Martin Baker ejection seats. The graduations on the in-flight refuelling probe provide a crude reversionary weapon-aiming system in the event of a strike sight failure. (*BAe Systems*)

was blessed with outstanding ground crew who worked long hours, often in the open and in foul weather, to sustain a flying programme of day and night flying and on countless exercises and detachments. Their affection for the aircraft was equal to that of those who flew it, and the mutual respect between air and ground crews was an endearing feature of the Buccaneer world in the Royal Navy and the RAF.

The most significant post-graduate course run by the OCU was the weapons instructor course. This was the brainchild of Honington's second Buccaneer Station Commander, Group Captain Peter Bairsto AFC. He had a long pedigree as a fighter pilot, including the command of a Hunter squadron, and he was a dedicated advocate of weaponry, formation leadership and tactics. He flew the Buccaneer regularly, in all its roles, and soon recognised the need for a specialist course to train a select number of crews to form a dedicated weapons and tactics cell within each operational squadron. This had been common practice on fighter squadrons some twenty years earlier, but the demise of the RAF Central Fighter Establishment had seen the end of this specialist training with the exception of the Pilot Attack Instructors (PAI) Course at the Hunter OCU, based at RAF Chivenor. The Royal Navy, however, had maintained their equivalent course, the very effective Air Warfare Instructor (AWI) Course. The Group Captain soon recognised that a 'bomber mentality' was building up around the use of the aircraft by the RAF and he was aware of the Royal Navy's use of the aircraft and their continued belief in the AWI Course. Given his own experience, he was convinced that a 'fighter ground attack attitude' for the Buccaneer force was more appropriate. At a presentation to senior officers at Headquarters Strike Command he made his famous remark: 'The Buccaneer is not a mini-Vulcan bomber but a maxi-Hunter FGA 9 and that is how we should operate it.'

His philosophy was given immediate credence during the discussion period that followed, when the first question posed by an air staff officer was 'where do you stow the sextant!!?' David Mulinder also drew comparison with the Hunter:

> The Buccaneer is first and foremost a superb aircraft. Custom-built for the task, it combines being a most effective means of delivering weapons with being great fun to fly. Descending from the rarefied atmosphere is analogous to being in a runaway lift but once at low level its true performance is obvious. Turbulence is shrugged off and the fuel lasts forever. As for weaponry, it is just like the Hunter but even better, being much more stable – and you could always blame the navigator for a poor bombing score!

The Buccaneer Attack Instructor (BAI) Course came into existence shortly afterwards and it continued to train weapons instructors for a further twenty-one years. Flight Lieutenant Jerry Yates, a former Hunter pilot who had also completed a Buccaneer tour with the Royal Navy, was tasked with developing and running the first BAI courses. He was an ideal choice for the appointment. He was an outstanding weapons pilot with a very imaginative and original approach to tactics. He had a detailed knowledge of the aircraft's weapon system and was always looking for modifications to make attack profiles more effective. He was able to instil his knowledge and enthusiasm into the thinking of his

Among the hard-working ground crew on every Buccaneer squadron, none worked harder than the armourers, seen here preparing to load a 1,000-lb HES bomb on the starboard inner pylon. The safety pins and their warning flags remain attached until the crew are ready to accept the aircraft. (*MOD/Crown Copyright*)

The standard route to the Wash weapon ranges took the Honington-based Buccaneers north to the Norfolk coast followed by a short transit over the sea to Holbeach or Wainfleet. These rocket-armed aircraft also carry unarmed practice bomb carriers on the remaining pylons. (*MOD/Crown Copyright*)

students, who invariably returned to their squadrons with a different perspective on tactics. His contribution to the operational effectiveness of the Buccaneer was considerable, and the subsequent award of the Air Force Cross for his work in developing the BAI course was both popular and well merited. Tragically, he was killed in a flying accident in Oman some years later.

The first BAI course commenced in March 1972 with three crews detached from their respective squadrons, usually as constituted crews, for the duration of the three-month course. Flight Lieutenant Dave Herriot, a navigator on XV Squadron, was one of the first students and he remembers the intensity of the course:

> Every day started early and finished late, whether it involved classroom lectures, phase brief preparation by the students or flying. Indeed, when the flying phase started, the days became even longer. As soon as one student-led sortie had been debriefed, the next day's lead crew would commence preparation for their mission. Sortie briefings had to be presented on the blackboard (yep, chalk and duster!) with all writing legible, evenly spaced and straight. Remember this was in the days when PCs did not exist, or at very best, were no further advanced than the Sinclair Spectrum! It was not uncommon to see BAI students burning the midnight oil, with chalk, ruler and duster in hand, attempting to correct the final points of their briefing before the 7.00 a.m. met brief the next day. Students quickly learned that an uneven curve on the depiction of the base-leg turn at Wainfleet Range was enough to raise comment by the staff before the sortie was even flown. No wonder the BAI course was referred to (by those who were not selected) as the **B**ullshit **A**nd **I**gnorance course. However, the efforts of the staff to ensure the very highest of standards were deliberate and, although some students failed to make the grade as BAIs, none failed to respond or appreciate the need to be

A 237 OCU aircraft carrying 2-in rocket pods on the inboard pylons. The Carrier Bomb Light Store, (CBLS) mounted on the outer pylons, replaced the practice bomb carriers; each carried two 28-lb practice bombs. The aircraft has the toned-down national markings. (*John Myers*)

> pressurised as a weapons instructor. Dropping live bombs is not an arcade game, and accuracy plus the utmost professionalism are required by all, but even more so by those who are instructors.

Following an initial mathematics revision course, the academic phase of the course included instruction in the calculation of sight settings, taking into account factors such as varying wind conditions, delivery profiles, release heights and dive angles. Knowledge of the Buccaneer weapon aiming system was, of course, essential and understanding the necessary calculations to ensure safe clearance between the aircraft, the ground and weapon detonation was imperative. The theory of 'flight path' weapons (bombs) and 'non-flight path' weapons (rockets/guns) was also taught. Terms such as ballistics, muzzle velocity, gravity drop (the effect of gravity on a weapon in flight), forward throw, time of flight and many more became routine to the BAI. A new lexicon had to be known and understood. The majority of this instruction was given by the 237 OCU weapon specialists, but lectures and briefings on the various weapon delivery methods were researched and conducted by individual students prior to each weapons sortie conducted on the local East Anglian bombing ranges using practice bombs. In addition to these events, BAI students conducted operational deliveries of rockets and live 1,000-lb HE bombs as the course advanced.

Most sorties to and from the bombing range would include field targets for Simulated Attack Profiles (SAP) whilst constantly being harassed by 'bounce' aircraft. The Fleet Air Arm had christened this latter activity 'strike progression', and thus it remained throughout the life of the Buccaneer, although other forces used the modern parlance 'evasion'. All BAI course sorties were flown as constituted four-ships with a staff crew flying in the number two position to assess the lead crew's performance. Debriefings were conducted immediately after landing and were never complete until the Strike Sight (HUD) film had been fully analysed with critical points assessed in minute detail and lessons learned discussed. Subsequently all, apart from the next day's lead crew, would retire to the bar to wash away any metaphoric bruising from the day's activities!

Once the standard weapon delivery profiles had been covered, the students were given individual projects to explore, and these included the assessment of new weapon delivery methods. Although projects were designed to exercise the students' knowledge, there were some significant spin-offs for the front-line squadrons, and new delivery profiles were introduced and subsequently became standard tactics and procedures. Flight Lieutenant Mike Bush of 12 Squadron was a pilot on the first course and he commented:

> Once all the various standard methods of attack had been flown, things started hotting up. Each student crew was given a weapon and an attack profile as a project and we had to work out weapon system settings, safe release parameters and flying techniques. My navigator and I were given 40° dive-bombing with the 1,000-lb bomb, never thinking that this non-standard attack would be used eighteen years later in the Gulf War. Ground school was fitted in between flying, and covered such subjects as evasive tactics against fighters and ground-to-air missiles, weapon effectiveness, electronic counter-measures, instructional technique and many others. After the ground school exam we concentrated on tactics. On every sortie a Hunter was used to 'bounce' the four-ship formation and occasionally Phantoms and Lightnings joined in the fun. Debriefs of these more complex sorties could take up to three hours – twice as long as the sortie! Throughout the

An unusual bomb load and configuration with a 1,000-lb HES on the starboard-inner and port-outer pylons. This aircraft has been modified with the bomb door fuel tank giving the aircraft a 'pregnant' look. The wing fold remained in constant use throughout the Buccaneer's service with the RAF. (*Peter March*)

Buccaneer pilots were rarely taken by surprise, but in this case perhaps a fighter has crept up unseen or the navigator has misbehaved. Almost certainly the latter since Buccaneer crews prided themselves on their lookout! (*John Plumb*)

> course the pressure remained at near breaking point and my wife once remarked that the BAI course was the best contraceptive on the market.

Once the value of the BAI Course had been recognised, similar courses were devised for the other RAF 'fast jet' squadrons, and the course was renamed the Qualified Weapons Instructor (QWI) Course.

Throughout the 1970s, anti-aircraft missile and gun defences became increasingly sophisticated and effective, so that attacking aircraft needed to limit their exposure time to a minimum if they were to survive. Unfortunately, in order to avoid debris damage to the attacking aircraft, the free-fall bomb had to be released from so great a height that the aircraft was very vulnerable to ground fire. The development of the Type 117 retard tail fitted to the 1,000-lb bomb gave rise to considerable discussion on methods of delivery, and this provided an ideal project for the QWI student crews.

Bomb fusing, debris avoidance, exposure times and target acquisition were the critical factors in deciding delivery parameters. In order to keep exposure time to a minimum the attack options rested between a level attack (laydown) and a shallow dive delivery. A toss attack would have been ideal but it was not sufficiently accurate against pinpoint targets and it remained as a defence suppression option only. Although the exposure time during a low-level attack was minimal, some targets were very difficult to acquire from 200 ft, particularly over land, and a level approach on a constant heading presented few problems to enemy gun defences. Early target acquisition was important and a shallow dive attack offered the pilot the best chance of successfully acquiring the target in time to manoeuvre the aircraft to achieve the necessary release parameters for an accurate attack. The QWI students addressed all these issues and flew numerous sorties and analysed the results, concluding that the most effective operational attack was a shallow dive using the retard bombs, which became known as the 'bunt retard' attack.

The advantages of the bunt retard attack were numerous. Attacking aircraft were exposed to enemy defences for the minimum time and the profile presented a manoeuvring target to defences. The dive gave good target acquisition and was the most accurate attack for the Buccaneer weapon system. There were some disadvantages. The pull-up from low level required a cloud base of 1,200 ft and the aircraft had to enter the target's defence engagement zone. Nevertheless, until the arrival of stand-off weapons, the attack was considered to be the primary precision attack, with level laydown attacks at 200 ft employed as a backup in the event of low cloud base.

In the bunt retard mode aircraft approached the target below 200 ft and at approximately two miles pulled up to 'tip in' on the target from 1,200 ft. The navigator became a talking altimeter as he called out heights every 200 ft, calling 'standby' at 700 ft and 'now' at 570 ft when the pilot released the bombs at 500 kts in an 8° dive and then immediately pulled 4 g to 10° nose up, before clearing the target and descending back to low level to escape.

The development of the bunt retard attack is a particularly good example of how the QWI Course could explore and analyse weapon delivery modes that subsequently benefited the front-line squadrons. Other courses developed night attack techniques, radar navigation overland and radar laydown bombing – all of which were subsequently adopted by the squadrons. Some years later No. 15 QWI Course had an opportunity to make a significant contribution to the development of a realistic self-defence capability for the Buccaneer force.

From the design stage there had been no plans to provide the Buccaneer with a self-defence capability and this was always seen as one of the few significant weaknesses of the aircraft. The Royal Navy had recognised the problem and, as the Scimitar was withdrawn from service, their Sidewinder AIM 9 B missiles were retained and the Buccaneer Mark 2s modified to carry the missile. With the demise of the final Royal Navy squadron these missiles were transferred to the

The Buccaneer's large internal bomb bay carried a variety of weapons including two nuclear stores, four Cluster Bomb Units or, as in this case, four 1,000-lb HE bombs. A 440-gallon fuel tank could be fitted in the bomb bay, and this was done for some long-range ferry sorties or when the aircraft was in the tanker fit. (*Mike Scarffe*)

The RAF Buccaneer force lacked a self-defence capability until surplus Royal Navy AIM 9-B Sidewinders were acquired in 1978. The first RAF squadron firing of a Sidewinder took place on 17 March 1987, when an AIM 9-G was fired during a detachment to RAF Valley. (*BAe Systems*)

RAF and were allocated to squadrons, but no RAF trial firings had taken place. In due course, the early-generation AIM 9-Bs were replaced with the improved AIM 9-G. In 1986 the OCU sought permission for the QWI Course to conduct a trial firing of the Sidewinder as their course project, and this was approved.

The firings were conducted on the Aberporth range, and three Buccaneers and a Hunter, together with thirty ground crew, deployed to RAF Valley. Flight Lieutenant Gary Stapleton of 237 OCU was one of the navigators and he takes up the story:

> This was the first time RAF squadron aircrew had fired a Sidewinder and the plan was to fire two missiles. The engineers were required to generate three Buccaneers and one Hunter for each sortie. The Buccaneers were all equipped with the Pavespike laser designator pod to enable the firings to be recorded on video. The range slot times allocated were thirty minutes and the primary firer and the Buccaneer and Hunter photo-chase aircraft entered the range with the secondary firer holding clear of the range in case it was needed. The target was a flare body towed by a Jindivik remotely-controlled pilotless aircraft. Speeds, heights and headings of all aircraft were controlled and recorded for analysis. To gain maximum advantage from the trial the first two sorties were 'dry', and this gave all those involved an opportunity to become familiar with procedures. For the two live firings, different profiles were flown from low level, with the firing aircraft having 100 knots overtake. The first was an astern firing against a non-manoeuvring target below, and the second, an abeam to stern firing against a manoeuvring target at the same height. Both firings were completely successful and the detachment was a great success.

Flight Lieutenants Mike Sullivan and Gordon Niven of 12 Squadron fired the first missile on 17 March 1987, and Flight Lieutenants Simon Smith of 208 Squadron and Gary Stapleton of 237 OCU fired the second. Not for the first time, the excellent ground crew achieved a 100 per cent aircraft serviceability rate. Following this highly successful trial the carriage of Sidewinder missiles became part of the standard war fit for Buccaneers.

The QWI Course was one of the great successes of the Buccaneer's RAF service and Mike Bush best sums up its value:

> The value of having a QWI pilot and navigator on each squadron soon became apparent, with a higher standard of briefing and debriefing, an improvement in weapons scores, better flying discipline, a higher standard of formation leadership and a better understanding and use of tactics. Squadron aircrew were encouraged to experiment with tactics and many standard operating procedures (SOPs) were reviewed. It wasn't long before other aircraft types set up their own QWI courses thus benefiting the whole of the RAF front-line squadrons. The concept of the QWI Course was a brilliant idea and was instrumental in creating an outstanding strike/attack force with the Buccaneer.

Not surprisingly, weapon training was fundamental for the Buccaneer squadrons and it figured on almost all sorties. From Second World War days, it had been a regular feature for attack squadrons to have a dedicated period of two or three weeks to concentrate entirely on weapons training by deploying to an Armament Practice Camp (APC). All Buccaneer squadrons spent three weeks each year at the NATO Air Weapons Installation at Decimomannu, in the south-west of the rugged island of Sardinia. The Italian Air Force administered the airfield and facilities and there were permanent support units from the RAF, German Air Force and USAF. Squadrons from each nation shared all the facilities, including the one air-to-ground weapons range at Capo di Frasca.

During most detachments there were squadrons from each of the three nations and the airfield and the weapons range were kept very busy. Coordination of the flying programme was

The busiest men during an Armament Practice Camp at Decimomannu were the armourers. A 2-in rocket pod is being re-loaded with up to thirty-six rockets. For training purposes, the rockets were normally fired as 'singles' from 900 ft in a 10° dive, when it was important to recover immediately to avoid ricochet damage. (*MOD/Crown Copyright*)

very tight and had to be strictly adhered to in order to give maximum utilisation of the time available on Frasca range. The Buccaneer squadrons were usually allocated four periods each day with four aircraft launched on each sortie, and this kept the ground crew, and the armourers in particular, very busy servicing and loading the aircraft with 68-mm SNEB rockets, 4-lb and 28-lb practice bombs (PB) and inert 1,000-lb HES (High Explosive Substitute) bombs. The weather factor was excellent and very few sorties were lost. As a result, most crews flew about twenty sorties, and this opportunity to concentrate almost exclusively on weapons training saw dramatic improvements in the accuracy achieved by the crews. Dave Herriot joined XV Squadron in 1972 just before the Squadron's first detachment to Decimomannu:

My first experience of Deci, as the base was affectionately known, was early in my first tour in July 1972. The squadron had re-formed with the Buccaneer only some nine months previously and this was the first time that the squadron had been away together as a 'team'. Weapon events in those early years of the Buccaneer in RAF service included dive-bombing with the 28-lb PB and 1,000-lb HES bombs, laydown with 4-lb PBs and rocketing with SNEB. All of these attacks were 'pilot-aimed'. Although regularly nagged by his back-seater, it was the pilot's responsibility to ensure that the aircraft was level at release on laydown attacks. However, dive attacks were heavily dependent on the navigator's ability to call out accurate heights in the descent to allow the pilot to assess the 'angle of dangle' in the dive. With only an analogue computer to aid the pilot with his weapon delivery, a poor dive angle or pitching at release could lead to the most horrendous bomb or rocket score. Nonetheless, the Bucc was very much a 'crew aircraft' and responsibility for shabby results was shared equally

Buccaneers of XV Squadron taxi out to Decimomannu's main runway. To avoid the risk of foreign object damage (FOD) to the engines, the aircraft taxied in a staggered formation either side of the taxiway centre line. (*Peter Rolfe*)

During the short transit to the Frasca weapons range, these XV Squadron aircraft practise some close formation. The miniature detonating chord (MDC) seen above the pilot's ejection seat fractured the canopy as he pulled the firing handle. The same system was fitted in the rear cockpit. (*Dick Cullingworth*)

at the subsequent sortie debrief; all feared the wrath of the QWI!

The day started early for the four crews detailed for the first sortie, with briefing at 7.00 a.m., one hour before take-off. After a briefing on the weather and local air traffic control procedures in force for the day, the formation leader briefed the conduct of the sortie, with particular emphasis on the formations to be flown in transit to and from the range, the weapon delivery modes to be employed and all the safety factors. Crews walked to their aircraft thirty minutes before take-off and, after start-up, the radios were checked with the leader and the four aircraft taxied to the runway in use. After a 'wind up' signal from the leader, engine rpm was increased and each pilot indicated that he was ready for take-off. The leader released the brakes and started his take-off roll, followed at ten-second intervals by the rest of the formation. The aircraft quickly joined up in a wide battle formation after take-off and departed for the range.

Frasca range was only 10 minutes' flying time from the airfield, and after a short low-level transit, the formation called the range safety officer on a discreet frequency as the four aircraft slipped into long line astern. The aircraft ran in individually at 200 ft and 500 kts and called 'finals live', and after clearance by the range safety officer, dropped a bomb in the laydown mode on the target, before pulling off hard to the left to join a racetrack pattern. Each bomb was armed with smoke and flash and the scores were calculated by the staff manning the quadrant huts and passed to each aircraft. The formation then settled to an orderly circuit, dropping weapons

Four aircraft of 12 Squadron join up in line abreast as they depart the Frasca range and transit back over the barren landscape of Sardinia. (*MOD/Crown Copyright*)

on each attack. If the pilot was not satisfied with the release parameters, he aborted the attack and continued until all eight bombs had been dropped. Once all crews had completed their attacks, the aircraft left the range and regained tactical formation, before setting off on a short low-level route through the rugged mountains at 420 kts. Forty minutes after take-off the formation arrived over the airfield in echelon and broke into the circuit to land. Once the aircraft had landed and been handed over to the ground crew for servicing and rearming, the crews gathered for debriefing.

One of the most important elements of any sortie was a detailed debrief. All aspects of the sortie were discussed in turn but emphasis was placed on a detailed assessment of each individual weapon score. Careful and robust analysis of each crew's results, and comparisons with other members of the formation, provided lessons for everyone. Use of the Telford 16-mm strike-sight camera allowed an accurate assessment of all the release parameters, such as dive angle, aiming and tracking and this explained many of the errors. Dave Herriott recalls one sortie flown by his Squadron Commander, Roy Watson, that caused some consternation at the debrief:

> On a very early trip to Frasca during our first detachment to Deci, our CO, who had flown Thunderjets during the Korean War and was a crack shot, was conducting rocket attacks and doing outstandingly well. Direct hit (DH) followed DH without a miss until, to the surprise of his navigator, he radioed to the RSO [Range Safety Officer] that he was 'Off dry' [no weapon fired]. When challenged by his navigator 'Why dry Boss, the parameters were perfect?' the Boss replied 'Sorry, I've just noticed that I haven't selected the sight glass up and the QWIs will bollock me rigid at the debrief!' In other words, he had fired the first rockets 'eyeballing' the target without using the aircraft weapon aiming system, yet all had successfully hit the centre of the target! A crack shot indeed.

Incidents abounded during a Deci detachment, and there are sufficient to fill a book. One of the more unusual and frightening occurred to Dave Herriot, but his reactions and the outcome typify much of the spirit and attitude of Buccaneer aircrew. He and his pilot, Iain Ross, were flying as the number four in a four-ship formation on a 20° dive-bombing sortie. As the pilot pulled into a 4 g turn at the top of the dive, Dave Herriot's ejection seat dropped two inches, disconnecting his personal equipment connector and so he was unable to breathe or communicate with his pilot. As the aircraft started the dive, Dave scribbled a note, 'bang seat dropped, can't breathe or speak', banged his feet to attract attention and squeezed the note through a myriad of black boxes to his pilot, who aborted the attack. Once downwind a note came back, 'never mind, we'll fly dry runs only!' Conscious that the seat might perform in the manner for which it was designed, a curt written reply was passed suggesting it might be more prudent to return and make an ultra-smooth landing. This was achieved to Dave's intense relief, but he was unceremoniously dumped at the end of the runway for fear that the seat would go off and the pilot taxied back to be met by an incredulous ground crew. Not wanting to walk back the two miles to the RAF dispersal, Dave managed to hitch a lift on the wing of a passing German F-104 and arrived back in some style. Such was the panache and camaraderie of crews deployed to Decimomannu. Dave Herriot experienced some of a different nature a few days later:

> Camaraderie even extended to the Italian Officers' Mess, where the aircrew of all four nations would mingle over dinner and in the bar afterwards. One evening we were talking to a group of Italian Air Force G-91 pilots about their techniques on Frasca. One of the Italians commented that he had been on duty as the range officer that day and had been intrigued by the Buccaneers carrying out 'divisional dive' bombing. This type of attack had been developed by the Royal Navy to gain the synergistic weight of effort on the same target. In short, two aircraft would dive on the target in close formation with the second crew dropping bombs on the leader's release. It required a great deal of practice but, if conducted well, could be highly effective. After copious international exchanges of 'round buying' including Deci Red, Grappa, flaming Sambucas etc., the processes and techniques of divisional dive-bombing were explained to the Italians. The next morning, the Buccaneers were taxiing for take-off. 'London formation, your mission eez cancel' said the local air traffic controller. 'Roger, reason why?' said London lead. 'The range, she is clos-edd' replied the controller. The Buccaneer formation taxied back and shut down irritated that our divisional dive sortie had to be aborted but we soon discovered why. Our G-91 pilot friends of the night before had got to the range earlier to practice divisional dive-bombing using our brief. Unfortunately, as they rolled into their first ever dive, they 'clapped hands' [collided]. Thankfully, they both survived their ejections and were back in the bar that evening for a bit of remedial instruction and another briefing.

Most squadrons devised a competition for the final day of the detachment, and ground crews could often be seen organising a sweepstake. Four bombs were released, the first from a first-run attack in the laydown mode, followed by a toss-bombing attack and then an 8° bunt retard dive attack. The final attack was a 'navigator's bomb'. The navigator's seat was slightly offset to the right and a little higher than the pilot's, giving him an excellent view over the pilot's right shoulder. After observing countless attacks, some navigators became very adept at assessing the weapon release points. The pilot flew the aircraft in a laydown attack and the navigator 'eyeballed' the target and released the bomb using a switch in the rear cockpit. It was not unusual for some navigators to better the score of their pilot!

* * *

After the frenetic activities typical of a Decimomannu APC, both in the air and on the ground, a peaceful flight home over the Alps gave the aircrew a chance to prepare for a return to domestic life at home. (*John Lillis*)

Air-to-air refuelling (AAR) was a daily occurrence for the UK-based squadrons and 809 Squadron, and training for crews commenced as soon as they arrived on their squadrons. The Buccaneer could be used as a tanker aircraft, and since 809 Squadron rarely had access to RAF tankers when embarked, the Squadron always kept at least one aircraft in the tanker fit, so crews posted to 809 carried out their training using the 'buddy-buddy' technique. Initial training for RAF squadron crews was carried out with the Victor tanker and, later, with its replacement, the VC 10, although buddy-buddy tanking was also practised. All tanker aircraft used the Mark 20c refuelling pod and so the techniques were identical.

As a tanker, the Buccaneer carried the refuelling pod containing 140 gallons on the starboard inner pylon, with a 250-gallon slipper tank on the port wing. An internal fuel tank was sometimes carried in the bomb bay and this could hold 440 gallons. From 1974 the Buccaneer carried the modified bomb door tank holding 425 gallons. With an internal fuel capacity of 1,560 gallons and the additional fuel carried in the auxiliary tanks, the Buccaneer was a very capable tanker aircraft.

Air-to-air refuelling operations were normally carried out above 20,000 ft, but heights could vary depending on air traffic control restrictions, high cloud and turbulence. Initial training was started at lower heights where the Buccaneer was more manoeuvrable and pilots flew their first sortie with an instructor in the back seat. GCI radar sites normally controlled the rendezvous with the Buccaneer approaching from below to formate on the port side of the tanker, at which point the tanker captain took over control of the formation. Once 'cleared astern', the Buccaneer moved across to the

The Buccaneer always carried the refuelling pod on the starboard inner pylon, and a 250-gallon wing tank on the port inner. A Tornado of TWCU, flown by former Buccaneer instructors, Flight Lieutenants Frank Waddington and Norman Roberson, has made contact and the fuel is flowing. (*Norman Roberson*)

starboard hose and stabilised about twenty yards astern waiting for clearance to 'close up'. The pilot then moved forward to 10 ft behind the basket and re-trimmed the aircraft. On the order 'clear dry' the pilot applied a small amount of power to achieve an overtake speed at walking pace using red reference lines on the underside of the tanker's wings to line up. It was important to resist the temptation to 'fly the basket' until the probe engaged the basket with a satisfying 'clunk'. If the basket was missed, it was important to reduce power immediately and start again. A trainee pilot would make two or three 'dry' engagements before being cleared 'wet'. On completion of the exercise the Buccaneer moved to the starboard side of the tanker and eased forward so that the tanker crew could see the aircraft. Squadron Leader Tony Lunnon-Wood describes the art of 'tanking':

> Basically it was a discipline and you had to keep it slow and orderly; don't rush into it, trim the aircraft carefully, and approach in stages. It was important to fly the probe into the basket by using the reference lines and try not to watch the basket, which had a natural movement and slight oscillations making it easy to get out of synchronisation and start to 'porpoise'. Once you started to chase the basket there was every chance that you would ram the probe through the spokes of the basket and damage either or both. In the debrief after the sortie there was no lying with tanking, you either got in or you didn't, and there was no way you could hoodwink anyone.

Air-to-air refuelling was a key aspect of Buccaneer operations for the UK-based squadrons. Crews practised regularly and became equally adept at night and when silent procedures were in force. The latter were controlled by the tanker crew through a series of lights on the rear of the refuelling pod. Buccaneer aircrew soon recognised that the tanker crews were a highly professional

An unusual customer for a Buccaneer tanker. This exercise was conducted at Boscombe Down during the evaluation of the Tristar. It did not become a regular feature of Buccaneer operations! (*MOD/Crown Copyright*)

force who gave an outstanding service, and there was a great deal of mutual respect.

A regular and popular annual feature was the appearance of the Buccaneer at many air shows. Since the early days of the Royal Navy squadrons, there were some outstanding display pilots and the aircraft was a regular on the air show circuit. By the mid-1970s, with squadrons regularly involved in exercises and overseas deployments, the commitment to display the aircraft was met by crews from the OCU. Flight Lieutenant John Myers had flown two tours on the aircraft when he joined the OCU as an instructor. He managed to persuade his Boss that he and his navigator, Flight Lieutenant Jim Crowley, were the perfect candidates for the 1978 season. By another inspired piece of flannel, he was able to stretch this to include the following year, and he takes up the story:

Like most pilots I enjoy flying aerobatics. Not only does it inspire confidence in one's ability in the air; it is also very rewarding and fun. Once my navigator, Flight Lieutenant Jim Crowley, and I had been selected, we decided the best way to proceed was to gain the advice and guidance of experienced Buccaneer display crews. Bruce Chapple was a mine of information, mentor and critical audience, whether we liked it or not. Quite correctly, he maintained that if anyone was going to display the Buccaneer they were representing the whole fleet, thus the crew concerned must perform professionally or they would answer to him! We were given the clearest and firmest of guidance at every stage of our work-up and during the display season, and it was made clear that there was no point in flying the 'best' display in the world unless it was safe. Every manoeuvre had to be guaranteed, predictable and flown as though the aircraft was 'on rails' and there must never be an element of improvisation – a proven killer of the inexperienced and unwary. These guidelines protected me throughout the future years of display flying, including my next tour of hundreds of air displays with the Red Arrows.

We developed a display profile that gave us an opportunity to show the aircraft in the best possible way. We arrived from 45° 'off crowd' at about 360 knots with the throttles almost closed as we crossed the display safety line to commence a max rate roll to 90° of bank, selecting full power on both engines. When parallel to the display line, snap roll to level flight and let the aircraft accelerate before snap rolling away from the crowd, now with the engines producing full power (and therefore lots of noise) before pulling up into a very high angle wing-over before flying over with everything 'hanging' and the bomb bay rolling open. After we had cleaned up, it was a series of slow rolls before accelerating to full power, with lots of smoke and noise at low level (officially 100 feet!), before disappearing vertically in a series of climbing rolls. In this way we were able to give our audience an appreciation of the splendid capabilities of the aircraft.

Our regular spare aircraft crew gave us magnificent service; post-display a very cold beer was always on hand as soon as we climbed out of the cockpit, but kept out of sight of the general public. Ken Alley and Scot Bergren, our tame USAF exchange officers, maintained their country's reputation for hospitality to the extreme. The term, 'party animals' immediately springs to mind when remembering them both. Many years later I am surprised that some people still remember and mention certain Buccaneer displays, usually ones flown in marginal weather. One in particular springs to mind, mainly because of its potential to wreck a number of careers – Crowley's and mine to mention just two! The very high profile Royal College of Defence Studies' course Air Day at RAF Waddington was one. The weather was very, very marginal but we didn't want to let the side down, so we flew the display in pouring rain, a low cloud base and poor to miserable visibility. Jim directed me round the pattern the whole time, giving instructions to tighten or slacken the turns in order to get on to the display line. I was fully occupied making sure we did not get too close to the ground. Later, back at Honington during the debrief in the Station Commander's office, his telephone rang. It was the AOC at Waddington wanting to

The Buccaneer was always a favourite on the air show circuit. With everything 'down' and turning hard in a moist atmosphere, it made an impressive sight and reminded onlookers of its naval heritage. The massive airbrake is very evident in this photograph of XX 901, which is now the property of the Buccaneer Aircrew Association and is on display at the Yorkshire Air Museum near York. (*Andrew Brookes*)

The photographic pack in the bomb bay always provided a good opportunity to 'advertise'. The camera installations are clearly seen in the forward part of the pack with the forward oblique housed in the blister. The rear of the pack held flares for night photography; it was never used but always formed part of the installation to maintain the centre of gravity. The Union Jack has inherited the fox of 12 Squadron's badge. (*Steve Fletcher, Flypast*)

congratulate him on providing the most outstanding and spectacular display of the day! It transpired that we were the ONLY display, as everyone else had decided to stay on the ground, apart from the Harrier who flew his 'vertical' display in one spot. Evidently the Buccaneer looked terrific when manoeuvring in such moist conditions with large persistent wingtip vortices streaming from the wings and the rear three-quarters of the fuselage shrouded in a thick cloud of pressure-wave condensation. As a gentle aside we were reminded not to 'push' the limits.

Years later, after leaving the RAF, people would assume my most enjoyable tour was the three years that I spent with the Red Arrows. They were somewhat surprised to learn that my most rewarding tour, professionally, was my three years' flying and displaying the Buccaneer with 237 OCU, although I must admit to having a fantastic time with the Reds.

John Myers and Jim Crowley performed with great professionalism and skill, but they would be the first to admit that they merely epitomised the panache of all those Buccaneer display crews that preceded them and others that were to follow. 'Spiv' Leahy and his team from 700Z Squadron led the way at Farnborough in 1962 and it ended thirty-two years later with the RAF's last Buccaneer display crew, Flight Lieutenants Glen Mason and Ian Donnelly.

CHAPTER 6

Maritime Operations

With the impending demise of the Royal Navy's fixed-wing carrier force, the RAF was tasked with providing tactical air support of maritime operations (TASMO) from land bases, in particular the attack of Soviet Navy Surface Action Groups (SAGs). The area of operations assigned to 12 Squadron was the Eastern Atlantic, from Gibraltar to the North Norwegian Sea. To cover this vast area, extensive use was made of air-to-air refuelling, and the Squadron regularly deployed to Forward Operating Bases (FOB) at Lossiemouth, Stornoway and St Mawgan, allowing the aircraft to extend its already long range even further.

When 12 Squadron formed in late 1969, the RAF had not been involved in the surface attack of warships since the Second World War days of the Coastal Command Beaufighter and Mosquito Strike Wings. The experiences of the Royal Navy squadrons provided an invaluable insight into anti-ship operations, but their attack formations would rarely exceed four due to limitations inherent in carrier-based operations. Land-based squadrons had the potential to mount much larger attack 'packages', and the initial tactics devised for the RAF maritime squadrons followed closely the principles of the tactics employed by the Strike Wings at the end of the war. Put simply, this was a defence suppression element followed by the precision attack sections.

By the late 1960s the increasingly sophisticated anti-aircraft defences of Soviet warships dictated that a stand-off weapon was needed for defence suppression and for precision attacks. The Martel missile was selected for RAF maritime squadrons and for the remaining Royal Navy squadron to provide a good stand-off capability, but in 1969 it was still a few years from entering service. The RAF decided not to use the Bullpup missile; so the tactics employed in the first few years were based on the use of the unguided conventional bomb and rockets.

The world's oceans cover vast areas and ships can easily disappear, presenting the first major problem to an attacking force – locating the target. Once 12 Squadron had completed an initial training programme to achieve a strike capability, it set about devising tactics to locate and attack surface ships. In November 1970 the largest RAF maritime exercise ever held took place in the Mediterranean, and 12 Squadron deployed ten Buccaneers to Luqa in Malta for Exercise 'Lime Jug'. Also participating in the exercise were the Victor photographic reconnaissance aircraft of 543 Squadron, and the two squadrons devised a system to identify target shipping based on continuous plotting of radar

When 12 Squadron re-formed with the Buccaneer in 1969, the RAF had not had a dedicated anti-shipping force since the Second World War. New tactics had to be devised and exercises with Royal Navy ships became a weekly occurrence for the next twenty-five years. This photograph was taken in 1970 and shows the Buccaneers carrying wing tanks for maximum range before the days of the bomb door tank. (*MOD/Crown Copyright*)

contacts. The technique was dubbed Continuous Radar Intelligence Surface Plot (CRISP). With their long endurance, the Victors maintained a continuous patrol of the exercise area, plotting all ship contacts. After a few hours a picture emerged that identified shipping on routine passage and others that were manoeuvring or operating as groups. The latter were then singled out, and their positions were passed by secure code to a Buccaneer probe aircraft flying a low probe (LOPRO) to identify potential targets. Once identified, the Victor shadowed the force, and by broadcasting the coded position continuously at regular and frequent intervals, the target could not determine when an attack was imminent. The Soviet Navy obliged by monitoring the exercise, and numerous 'interceptions' were made against Soviet warships, providing invaluable experience for the crews new to maritime operations. Flight Lieutenant Jon Ford was impressed:

> A Soviet *Kashin* class destroyer was anchored about thirty miles out on the centre line of the main Luqa runway. It was a formidable looking ship and became the recipient of many low-level fly-bys. Rumour had it that the captain sent a signal of complaint at the behaviour of these 'Navy' jets to the Captain of *Ark Royal* who replied with a curt one-liner 'If you do not want to play, go away'. A few days later a shadowing Soviet *Kotlin* class destroyer made a mess of a turn and collided with the *Ark*. A few days later we took off for a long-range sortie in order to build up the monthly hours. David Mulinder was unable to retract the undercarriage and, mindful of the Squadron Commander's edict about flying hours, he spent the next two hours circling the *Kashin* with undercarriage and hook down whilst taking photographs. There is no record of what the Soviet captain thought.

The Soviet Navy maintained a close watch on activities during Exercise 'Lime Jug'. In doing so, they provided an ideal opportunity for 12 Squadron crews to carry out visual, photographic and radar reconnaissance. Two Buccaneers are investigating this SAM Kotlin, but strict rulings dictated that aircraft must not approach closer than 400 yards or make aggressive manoeuvres. The opportunity to face a 'potential enemy' was one of the great benefits of the maritime scene. (*MOD/Crown Copyright*)

The method of 'shadow support', devised during 'Lime Jug', formed the basis of more refined tactics over the next twenty years. Vulcans of 27 Squadron were tasked exclusively with maritime radar reconnaissance. Their crews became expert at identifying targets in a cluttered sea area and new methods of passing coded dispositions were developed. Canberras and Buccaneers flying LOPRO sorties were often launched to identify the targets. Shackleton AEW aircraft were sometimes used to provide Tactical Direction (TACDI) when they used their radar to identify both the target and the Buccaneer attack formations before directing the Buccaneers to their targets. This was a secondary role for the Shackleton. With the demise of the Vulcans in 1982, the Nimrod MR 2, equipped with the Searchwater radar, assumed the task, and with its other sophisticated aids, it was able to provide a verbal surface picture (SURPIC) and give accurate range and bearing information of the target. Under certain circumstances the Nimrod was able to vector the Buccaneers direct to the target.

With large areas of ocean devoid of enemy activity, the standard profile adopted by a Buccaneer maritime attack formation was a

Buccaneers of 12 Squadron share the flight line with Phantoms of 43 Squadron at Luqa, Malta, during Exercise 'Lime Jug' held in November 1970, the first major RAF maritime exercise for both recently formed squadrons. (*MOD/Crown Copyright*)

Hi-Lo-Hi. This had the added advantage of extending the range to as much as 600 miles' radius without refuelling, and this range was regularly extended by the use of air-to-air refuelling. Whenever possible, formations were made up of six or eight aircraft, and during the transit to the target area in wide battle formation, all the crews listened out on the radios for the latest information on target locations. All aircraft maintained radio and radar silence to avoid giving away their approach to a target. At a range of 240 miles from the target the Buccaneer formation started an 'under the radar lobe' descent to sea level in order to stay outside the enemy's radar cover. During the descent the passive radar warning receiver was monitored for selected search radar frequencies, and if one was detected, the rate of descent was increased to remain outside the detection range. At 30 miles the leader 'popped up' and the navigator switched on his Blue Parrot radar for two or three sweeps, during which time he identified and 'marked' the target before descending back to 100 ft. The lead navigator then had to inform the rest of the formation and this created problems. Flight Lieutenant Bruce Chapple was 12 Squadron's QWI and he explains how the problem was resolved:

> After choosing the radar return that was assessed to be the 'high value target', the leader attempted to convey the information verbally over the radio to the rest of the formation. The plan sounded good in principle, but had some drawbacks, not least the ambient noise in the cockpit at high speeds, which made it difficult to understand all but the simplest messages. This was exacerbated when a senior navigator on the squadron insisted on his own solution – a lengthy dissertation over the radio describing what he could see on his radar screen. After a particularly 'lively' debrief, it was suggested from the floor, that perhaps the situation might be improved if the attack message was passed by someone with 'more than half a brain and without a speech impediment!' During this period, the US Navy exchange officer, Lieutenant Bill Butler, suggested quietly that if the Doppler-stabilised radar track marker was used, and a suitable range ring was selected on the radar, the lead aircraft could turn to put the most likely radar return on the track marker line (the rest of the formation paralleled the leader's heading), and fly it down the track marker line until the range return coincided with the range ring, all that was needed was a simple codeword recognisable even in poor radio conditions to convey the mark to the formation. This suggestion was taken up, tried in the air, and found to be a brilliant, simple and consistent solution. The codeword? 'Bananas!' It was never changed, and it became the trademark attack call of the Buccaneer force – usually followed by a split!

At the pre-sortie briefing one of a number of 'Alpha' attack profiles designed to provide a multi-axis coordinated attack was selected as the primary option depending on the defences of the planned target. The leader could change the option at short notice if weather or enemy ship dispositions dictated different tactics, and the new 'Alpha' attack was broadcast with the 'Bananas' call. Radio transmissions were kept to an absolute minimum. Accelerations were never called but were based on the leader's 'smoke emissions' from the engines. All turns were with 60° of bank and timing started from the beginning of the turn. In total radio silence 'Bananas' was not called, but the leader rocked his wings and the split was executed as soon as the leader started his turn. Flight Lieutenant David Wilby was a navigator on 12 Squadron and he was involved in developing the 'Alpha' attacks:

> The aim of the Alpha attacks was to maintain the element of surprise for as long as possible by descending outside the radar horizon of the enemy ship by initiating a series of pre-planned geometric splits, to confuse the target defences and delay the lock-on solutions for their radar-laid anti-aircraft defences. Formation sizes were normally six to eight, depending on the target, although weather conditions or night operations sometimes reduced the optimum to a more manageable size to suit the prevailing conditions. Once we had penetrated target ship's weapons engagement zones, we used the exceptional low-flying performance of the Buccaneer to fly at

high speed and ultra-low level and still be able to sustain high-g manoeuvres to increase the tracking problems of the enemy radars. The first attacks were delivered from a toss delivery at three miles on converging headings. Each bomb was fused to explode at sixty feet, with the aim of destroying the fire-control radars and incapacitating the missile and gun crews. In the meantime, the attack force had turned starboard through ninety degrees before rolling in to release four to six 1,000-lb bombs independently from a low-level dive or laydown attack that provided the killing blow. Timing was critical if aircraft were to avoid the debris from the preceding attack. The obvious weakness of this attack was the vulnerability of the aircraft – particularly those that carried out the precision attack.

ALPHA ATTACK PROFILE

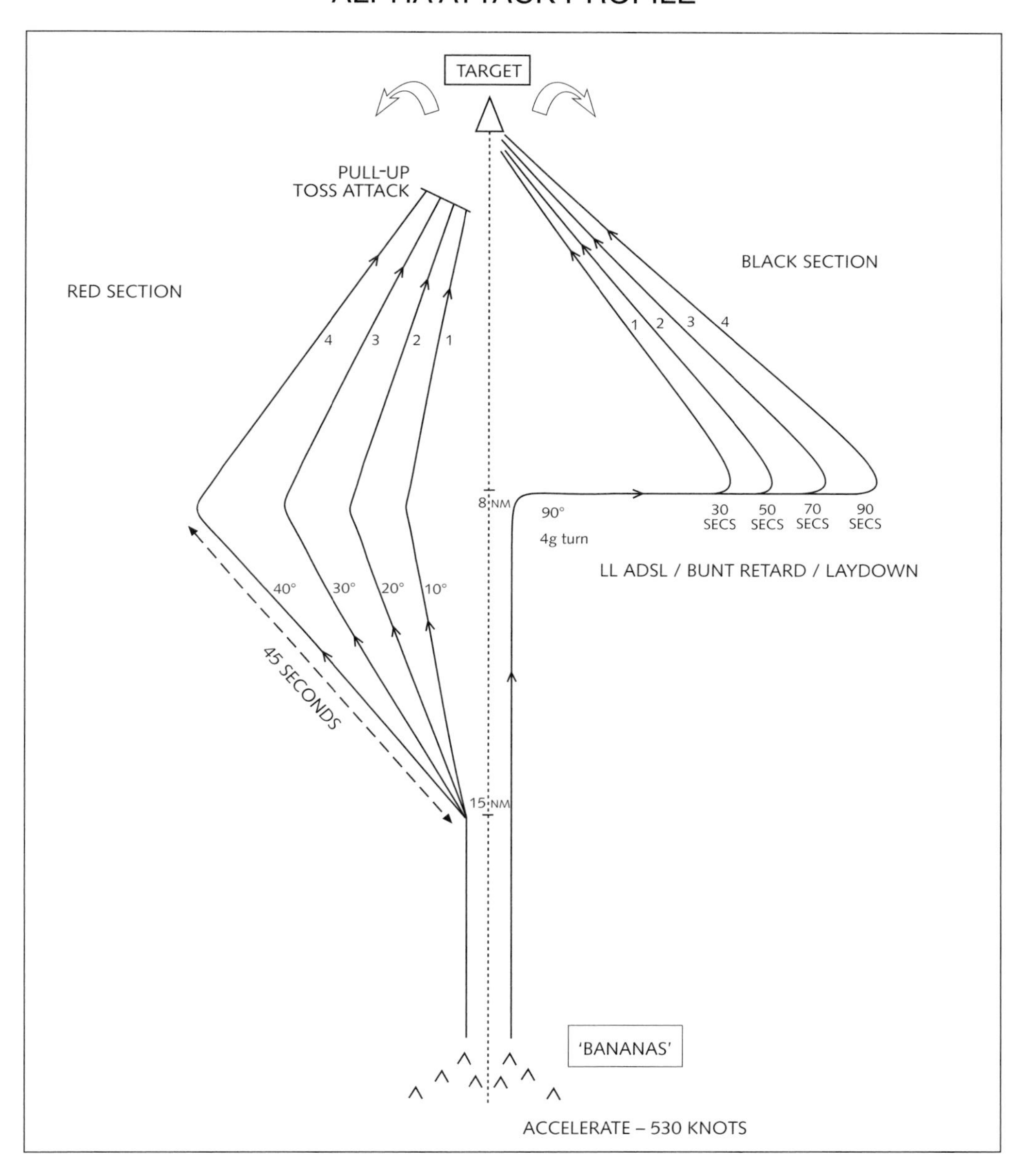

This diagram outlines the basic 'Alpha' coordinated attack profile. There were numerous other options but all based on this same principle.

Coordinated attacks were also practised at night, but with formations of four aircraft operating at a minimum height of 200 ft, which required considerable concentration. The principle was similar to the day profiles, but the precision low-level bombing was avoided and the preferred delivery mode was medium toss, giving a degree of 'stand-off'. There were two periods that required particular attention. The first was the 4 g recovery from the toss delivery, which required 135° angle of bank, until the nose passed through the horizon, when the bank was reduced to 90° and the aircraft dived for the sanctuary of low level. The second was the formation rejoin in the very dark conditions, which was time-consuming and disorientating.

Less well-defended targets, such as FPBs, were attacked using Lepus illumination flares thrown by the lead aircraft of a pair. As they approached the target, the No. 2 aircraft dropped astern when the cloud base dictated the trail distance. The lower the cloud, the later the 'flare show', and so the trail distance had to be increased. The leader tossed the flares to deliver them ahead of, and beyond, the target and the second aircraft attacked with SNEB rockets or, occasionally, bombs, with the target silhouetted in the light lane created by the flares. Bruce Chapple explains the rest of the attack:

Whilst the No. 2 attacked using a shallow dive profile, the leader regained control from the toss delivery and made a follow-up attack behind the No. 2. During the toss recovery, a great amount of hands flashing round the cockpit took place – a prime situation for disorientation – in order to select switches for the next attack. During this interesting whirling dervish act, the No. 2 took the lead and flew a racetrack pattern and made a second flare delivery followed by the leader. What made life particularly interesting during the attack was that

A non-tactical formation of 12 Squadron Buccaneers as they jettison fuel in unison. A low-level-float switch in each of the four main fuel tanks prevented the inadvertent dumping of all the fuel in the unlikely event that the pilot forgot to switch off the fuel jettison switch. (*MOD/Crown Copyright*)

> the three flares were given different 'flare height settings', which meant that they were not in a horizontal line or in line with subsequent dive attacks. In addition, there always seemed to be one at twelve o'clock high during the 5 g recoveries from the dive attacks. All very disorientating! One night, during an exercise in the Baltic, one pair managed to get six flares burning at the same time, i.e. four attacks in four minutes! The FPBs were suitably baffled as was the innocent shipping in the Skagerrak.

During the mid-1970s, 809 Squadron had an establishment of fourteen Buccaneers and flew from HMS *Ark Royal* and from Honington when disembarked. The Squadron took part in many exercises and all these involved intensive weapons and tactics training. An intensive weapons training period was conducted at the Roosevelt Roads Weapons Training Area off Puerto Rico in January 1975. Over 1,500 rockets were fired and after dropping 170 practice bombs, 40 1,000-lb HE bombs were released, including some in toss attacks at night when the target was illuminated by Lepus flares. During exercises off Florida, 40° dive-bombing was investigated and the period was concluded with the first firing of an AIM-9B Sidewinder air-to-air missile fired by Lieutenant Mike Sharp against a towed target 5,000 ft behind a drone on his last sortie in the Royal Navy. The Squadron continued to practise attacks against ship targets, and Tony Ogilvy makes an interesting comment on the attack philosophy of 809 Squadron:

> By the mid-1970s the worth of the ultra-low ingress and egress was still the ideal attack profile for attacking ships. I remember the different approach to tactics between the RN and the RAF that emerged at Honington, with 12 Squadron adopting

the large formation for saturation attacks and the smaller four-ship attack formations favoured by the RN. Of course, our approach was governed as much by the realities of deck versus land operations as by tactical advantage. I could clearly see the benefit of the physics of overpressure/blast/fragmentation generated by a large formation making a co-ordinated attack. But I also saw first hand that, unless this form of attack was practised to near perfection, the loss of synergistic advantage through mis-timing was considerable and you had all your eggs in one basket. We learned a lot from the RAF and the USN and modified our tactical thinking to a degree, but the basic principle of initial stand-off to suppress defences before the attack team went in held up for the majority of heavily-defended targets. However, given the development of the air defence systems deployed with the Soviet Fleet, it was becoming clear that to enter the fifteen mile air-defence envelope of the primary target was unhealthy and a stand-off missile was a 'must' for the initial engagement.

The answer to the need for a stand-off weapon was the Martel missile, which was available with either a TV seeker and radio command guidance or a passive radar homing seeker. Martel was one of the first Anglo-French military collaborative projects, with the French primarily responsible for the development and evaluation of the Anti-Radiation (AR) version and the UK having similar responsibilities for the TV missile system. The AJ 168 TV-guided missile became the primary attack weapon for the maritime Buccaneer force. Aircraft required a substantial modification to carry the missile, including the installation of new weapon pylons and a cockpit display and stick controller for the navigator. The display was a television screen placed between the navigator's legs – an uncomfortable posture, as Flight Lieutenant Jim Boyd discovered on a six-hour proving flight! The TV version of the missile was 12 ft 9 in and had a launch weight of 1,146 lb with a 350-lb semi-armour piercing, radar-fused warhead to penetrate ship's hulls. The solid propellant motor gave a range of 15 miles. The missile flew a predetermined mid-course trajectory at about 2,000 ft, which was necessary for target acquisition and to maintain the data

There are few photographs of Buccaneers carrying Lepus flares. Two were carried on a tandem beam. This 809 Squadron aircraft is also carrying two 540-lb HES bombs on a tandem beam. The 540-lb bomb was very rarely used in the RAF. (*P.H.T. Green*)

link with the launch aircraft. TV imagery from the missile's camera was relayed back to the navigator by the data link, which then transmitted control inputs made by the navigator using the small control stick.

The missile was launched from the delivery aircraft at 100 ft and 500 knots at 15 miles range from the target, and after release, the weapon climbed to its mid-course phase. The navigator could descend the missile to stay below cloud and he was able to pan the camera left and right to facilitate early target acquisition, which was dependent on the visibility. Once visual with the target, which ideally would be when it appeared at the top of the TV screen, the navigator would wait until it reached halfway down, when he selected terminal phase, giving him full control of the missile's flight. He maintained the cross wires over the aiming point by giving up/down and right/left commands with his control stick. The point at which the terminal phase was selected was critical. Too far from the target resulted in a long shallow approach, which was difficult to control in the last few seconds before impact. Too close to the target resulted in a rapid nose-down command to the missile, giving a very short time of controlled flight.

The firing programme for the evaluation of TV Martel began with a launch in February 1970 and was completed in July 1973 when the twenty-fifth missile was fired. Trials were carried out by No. 22 Joint Services Trials Unit operating from A&AEE Boscombe Down, but using Aberporth for live firings. No. 12 Squadron flew the first in-service trials in October 1974 and the lead navigator was Flight Lieutenant Mick Whybro, one of the most experienced RAF Buccaneer navigators. He describes the pre-trial training:

> Before the trial started the navigators had to complete hundreds of runs in the Terminal Phase Simulator. This presented them with just about every possible situation they could find themselves confronted with when selecting terminal phase. Late target acquisition, target too far left or right, varying dive angle conditions, missile control problems and various crosswind conditions could all be practised. In addition, aircraft were fitted with a TV Airborne Trainer (TVAT), which was virtually the TV part of the missile mounted on the starboard inner pylon. During routine training sorties, the navigators could select a suitable ship target and practise the tracking. The navigator could steer the pilot as though he was flying the missile and talk him down to a successful attack with the break-off from the ensuing dive at the pilot's discretion!
>
> Pilots could practise the breakaway manoeuvre flown after the missile launch. This was a 3 to 4 g level turn at launch height away from the target but ensuring that the data link pod remained on the target side of the aircraft. The turn continued through 120°, when the aircraft rolled out and maintained heading until the missile impacted. On the actual firing run the navigator would experience this breakaway manoeuvre with the sea streaking past his left ear at 100 ft in a 4 g turn while his TV screen told him that he was straight and level at 1,500 ft, which could be a little disturbing.

A TV Martel anti-shipping missile is carried on the port inner pylon with the data link pod carried on the starboard inner. The Wide Band Homer aerials are prominent outside the empty outer pylons. (*Dave Herriot*)

The solid-propellant motor of the Martel fires as the missile is released by the low-flying Buccaneer. (*Norman Browne*)

The first trial was supervised by the Central Trials and Tactics Organisation (CTTO) and was very carefully controlled in order that all the safety factors could be adhered to. The target was a 30-ft long raft with a vertical structure containing the aiming point. Six missiles were fired and all scored direct hits. The second trial took place twelve months later and the aircraft were given more tactical freedom for the launch phase. Mick Whybro relates the events:

> As with the previous year, the trial was successful but, this time, only five direct hits were achieved with the six firings. The missile that missed the target was quite spectacular nonetheless! CTTO decided to run a joint trial, which was designed to evaluate the Phantom's radar performance in acquiring and tracking a TV Martel in a head-on attack. Apparently the Phantom acquired the missile successfully after release. However, the Martel on that particular launch did not perform with the same degree of success! The navigator, Ken MacKenzie, selected 'terminal phase' but found that he had no elevation control over the missile, which went into a steep climb. There was a complete blanket of cloud between 2,000 and 5,000 ft over the range and Ken had a clear picture of the missile entering cloud and emerging in to the clear air above. He then saw a dark blur, which was the Phantom at very close range. The 43 Squadron pilot had the shock of his life when a large telegraph pole shot vertically in front of his nose at a very uncomfortable range! The range controller decided it was time to destroy the errant Martel before it could do any serious damage.

AR Martel was a lock-before-launch missile of similar proportions to the TV variant, which could be fired from high level with a maximum range of 30 miles or from 200 ft at a range of 15 to 20 miles. Two Buccaneers of 12 Squadron deployed to the French Air Force base at Cazaux, near Bordeaux, for a four-week in-service trial in September/October 1974, with missile firing taking place on the nearby Biscarosu Range. Squadron Leader Colin Cruikshanks and Flight Lieutenant David Wilby successfully fired a missile on 11 September 1974 from 19 miles,

A Buccaneer of 12 Squadron has a full complement of Martel missiles. TV versions are carried on the port inner and starboard outer pylons, and the associated data link pod is on the starboard inner. An anti-radar version is carried on the port outer pylon. (*Dave Herriot*)

flying at 200 ft and 550 kts – and registered a hit. A second missile exploded in flight, but the problem was resolved and the trial concluded with another successful hit on 15 October.

Two radar seeker heads were available for the missile. One operated in the band optimised to detect the Soviet Navy's most advanced long-range search radar, the Topsail. The other operated in the band more commonly fitted to the Headnet C search radar used by many Soviet warships. Seeker heads could be set for a particular target frequency and sector-scanned for radar acquisition, or the seeker head could be fixed and the frequency swept to gain a lock-on. Extremely good sensitivity gave excellent detection with audio and visual indications and this made the missile an excellent warning receiver and gave the aircraft an 'electronic range' advantage, enabling the Buccaneer to fly its 'under the lobe' descent to remain outside target detection range until very close to missile launch. After launch the missile remained locked to the target frequency and was boosted to around 15,000 ft following a homing profile, which eventually put it into a steep terminal dive at around Mach 2 to detonate a proximity-fused blast warhead of 350 lb just above the target with the aim of degrading a ship's primary surveillance radars. With the target 'blinded', the following aircraft with their precision weapons had a much greater chance of survival. Someone neatly summed up the tactic as, 'We first poke them in the eye, then we knee them in the balls.'

During April 1975 one of the Soviet Navy's latest and most potent cruisers, the *Kresta II*, equipped with the 'Topsail' radar, transited the North Cape of Norway into the North Norwegian Sea. This presented an ideal opportunity to assess the accuracy of the AR Martel's seeker head, and 12 Squadron were cleared to fly four sorties to try and locate the cruiser and obtain data. David Wilby flew three of these sorties and recounts the details:

To maintain the element of surprise, and our aircraft's identity, all Buccaneer emitters including the Blue Parrot radar, Doppler and Tacan were switched off throughout the flight and we also maintained radio silence. A dedicated Victor tanker refuelled us north of the Faroes on our outbound leg and waited to rendezvous with us on our return. The first sortie was designed to test the procedures, but we had very poor and old data on the position of the target. However, it was detected at long range and a rough position was calculated. On the second flight I flew with the Squadron Commander, Wing Commander Graham Smart, and I detected the target and we homed for a visual confirmation under a 200-ft cloud-base with less than a mile visibility some 900 miles north of the Shetlands – a long way from home. Recovery weather in the UK was Red [below minimums] and the tanker had to leave the final rendezvous early and divert to Lossiemouth, which was also Red. It was a good job my Bingo fuel

The leader of a six-ship Alpha attack against shipping fired AR Martels to put enemy radars out of action, before the precision attacking force dropped their weapons. This aircraft carries two AR Martels and a Westinghouse ALQ 101-10 ECM pod for self-protection on the port outer. (*Author's collection*)

An unusual 'target' for this Buccaneer was HM Yacht *Britannia.* Fortunately Her Majesty was not on board! Former Buccaneer pilot Rear Admiral Sir Rob Woodard was Captain of the Yacht, and he agreed to a 'visit' as the ship sailed off the Hebrides. (*'Pony' Moore*)

A TV Airborne Trainer (TVAT) was developed to give crews an opportunity to practise target acquisition and dummy attacks against any ship. It used a streamlined Martel seeker head and was mounted on the same rear-raked inner pylon that carried the TV data link pod. After acquiring the target, the Buccaneer simulated the missile profile and overflew the target ship. This aircraft also carries an ALQ 101-10 ECM pod. (*Jelle Sjoerdsma*)

> of 14,500 lb was accurate and it allowed us to recover from the target near Jan Mayen Island to Lossiemouth to land and refuel after a six-hour flight before recovering to Honington. After a further triangulation sortie, I flew with Dave Ray when the weather conditions were good and we were able to detect, home to and photograph the target. I expect the captain of the *Kresta* was surprised to see a Buccaneer in such northern latitudes, but it gave all of us on 12 Squadron a lot of confidence in the capability of the missile.

October of 1975 saw the third and final TV Martel trial firings at Aberporth when 809 Squadron fired a number of missiles. With both missiles well proved, they became a standard weapon load for 12 and 809 Squadrons and attacks with Martel became the primary attack option. Nevertheless, whatever the weapon loads carried on each wing, aircraft were always loaded with four free-fall or retard 1,000-lb bombs in the bomb bay. This was a significant bonus and provided numerous attack options, depending on the target or any changing tactics it might employ. The Apha tactics were modified to take advantage of the stand-off capability of the missiles. The Alpha Six was an all-missile attack against a target that continued to transmit with its search radar and AR missiles were fired at 10 miles, followed by a TV attack by aircraft immediately behind. If the target switched off its radar, an Alpha Seven attack was flown with four aircraft accelerating to 540 knots and splitting outwards in pairs at 15 miles to toss the bombs on different attack headings. In the meantime, the remaining aircraft decelerated to 360 knots and fired a TV missile each, at 10 miles, to provide the lethal attack. At night, when the TV missile was ineffective, AR missiles were fired, followed by a section tossing bombs at the target.

TV Martel gave good service for the next ten years and AR Martel went on to be an integral part of Buccaneer anti-ship attacks, providing excellent target detection for setting up an attack and giving a first-class defence suppression capability. It remained in operational service until the retirement of the Buccaneer in 1994.

No amount of routine daily training could compensate for the lack of opportunities to practise operational tactics under realistic conditions. The maritime environment offered greater scope and the regular large-scale exercises did provide good training. There were few restrictions over the sea, and sophisticated, heavily armed warships of the NATO navies provided very realistic 'targets', and both 12 and 809 Squadrons were in constant demand as enemy and as allies, and exercise scenarios were developed that gave the Buccaneer squadrons ample opportunity to practise tactics in a 'hostile' environment. A major NATO maritime exercise, lasting two weeks, took place every autumn and often involved up to twenty warships and submarines and hundreds of aircraft in various roles. Smaller exercises were a regular feature of the maritime squadron's annual training programme, and Buccaneers were in constant demand to provide targets for individual warships fulfilling their own training requirements. Ships manoeuvred and activated their own radars and fire-control systems and most deployed a 'splash' target, thus providing mutual benefit for the Buccaneers.

All Buccaneer aircrew became very familiar with the courses run by the Joint Maritime Operational Training Staff (JMOTS) based at RAF Turnhouse, near Edinburgh. Joint Maritime Courses (JMC) became a regular feature for over thirty years and provided valuable training. Although the JMC was a national course, participation by invited NATO ships and aircraft allowed joint procedural training and provided the Buccaneer squadrons with different and realistic targets. After a series

Exercises organised by the Joint Maritime Operational Training Staff (JMOTS) took place two or three times each year, and Buccaneers were in constant demand as targets for Royal Navy ships and as an attack force against the 'enemy'. (*MAP*)

of discussion periods, ships sailed from the Firth of Forth and immediately came under air attack as basic tactics and procedures were practised. Buccaneers were in constant demand as 'targets', providing ship's operations staff, missile and gun crews with a very potent and realistic target. Once the naval force was in position north of Scotland, the exercise moved into a five-day combat phase representing the transit of an Anti-Submarine Task Group through the United Kingdom Air Defence Region (UKADR) towards Norway or the Shetland Islands. The ships moved along a predetermined track designed to ensure maximum interaction with submarines, maritime patrol aircraft and attack aircraft.

The early JMC exercises in the 1970s provided an ideal scenario for 12 Squadron to develop tactics and procedures for a role that had not been practised by the RAF since World War Two. It was a steep learning curve and the aircrew often felt that the 'bomber' syndrome of the air staffs stifled their initiative. However, as experience was gained and more Buccaneer aircrew filled important staff appointments on completion of their flying tours, the full capability of the Buccaneer became more accepted, the support of higher formations was excellent and the quality of training improved significantly. The JMC exercises themselves became more sophisticated and responded quickly to developments and the changing capabilities and tactics of the Soviet Navy. Exercises held in the late 1980s generated almost 500 attack sorties flown against surface naval forces and conducted in a heavy Electronic Warfare (EW) environment. 'Force packages' of Buccaneers, with escorting fighters and jamming aircraft, formed part of raids by over fifty aircraft. The Buccaneers made extensive use of air-to-air refuelling and Nimrod aircraft provided targeting information and attack direction. Wing Commander Graham Smart MBE AFC recalls his time commanding 12 Squadron:

> A tour as OC 12 Squadron was certainly the highlight of my operational life. It coincided with

what was a very exciting time in the evolution of the Buccaneer's operational life. None of the restrictions of the carrier deck, a much more reliable aircraft and a new range of weapons, including the TV and AR versions of the Martel missile. The introduction of Martel radically affected the whole maritime attack concept. The weapons provided a true stand-off capability, with a degree of accuracy hitherto entirely outside the capability of the Buccaneer force, thereby increasing flexibility and economy in its utilisation.

In the maritime role we had the opportunity to train over the seas that we would have had to fight over, and the exercises were virtually the real thing except the air defence systems were not firing at us. We employed the same tactics that we would use in war, flying at the same heights and speeds, listening to real radars, searching for real ships and often coming face-to-face with the powerful Soviet Navy. There were also huge benefits for the NATO navies in having the Buccaneer as an 'enemy', since we presented them with a very elusive and realistic threat they had to counter. In this environment we were constantly assessing and developing new tactics and able to train exactly as one would fight in war – perfect!

The Squadron was worked very hard but nobody seemed to mind, although the odd spouse may have disagreed – detachments to unlikely places and exercises galore. We went back to what was by then RAF Lossiemouth, a forward operating base for most of the major maritime exercises – a routine of sleep, eat, brief, fly, debrief, eat and sleep for two weeks – no alcohol, but a good party afterwards and exactly what we would have done in war. A host of memories; chasing a new *Kresta II* off Bear Island in a blizzard, tossing Lepus flares against a frigate miles north of the Shetlands on a stormy November night, with three others in tow and hoping they were hanging in, chasing fast patrol boats in the Norwegian fjords and weekend exercises off Gibraltar providing targets for the Navy. Two and a half great years, most of us probably neglecting wives and children a little – after all being at home meant that you were probably missing something!

The greater survivability created by the stand-off capability of Martel was further enhanced by the introduction of the Westinghouse ALQ 101-8 ECM pod carried on an outer wing station. This provided noise and repeater jamming programmes with a cockpit control unit allowing selections to be made to combat a particular threat. In 1974 the ARI 18228 radar-warning receiver (RWR) was introduced. In essence, the RWR detected radar transmissions using two combined aerial units mounted fore and aft in the bullet fairing at the top of the fin. Each aerial unit comprised three paired receivers, operating in the 2.5 to 18 GHz range, for both pulsed and continuous wave (CW) transmitters. The aerials were mounted at right angles and, by comparing the phase of each received radar signal, the relative bearing of the source could be measured. The overlapping fields of view of each aerial unit provided 360° cover and bearing accuracy was excellent for all pulsed signals. The characteristics of CW radars were such that an accurate bearing could not be measured by the RWR. In this case, only the related quadrant would be indicated to the Buccaneer crew. Pulsed signals were displayed on a cathode-ray tube in real time, and an audio signal was generated on the intercom, providing the crew with indications of the frequency, aerial rotation rate and relative strength of the received signals. The availability of directional information, audio

The maritime squadrons made increasingly frequent detachments to the USA where there were excellent weapons and electronic warfare range facilities. Two Buccaneers of 12 Squadron are framed by a resident RA-5C Vigilante during an exercise at US Naval Weapons Centre at China Lake in California. (*Peter Rolfe*)

recognition and a threat warning alarm allowed the navigator to identify the threat and make appropriate settings on the ECM pod to counter it. The RWR provided a much greater capability than the old wide band homer (WBH), housed in bullet fairings on each wing leading edge, although these were retained for its capability against certain Soviet Navy search radars.

The Buccaneer pioneered the introduction of tactical electronic warfare systems in the RAF, and this electronic warfare suite gave excellent service and greater tactical flexibility for the next decade before it was upgraded. Flight Lieutenant Vic Blackwood carried out much of the early work devising tactics:

> Once familiar with the RWR, and after our early work with ships, we turned our attention to countering an airborne threat. Roaming the east coast was bread and butter to Buccaneer squadrons and it seemed logical to ask the Binbrook Lightning squadrons to participate in our early attempts. The Lightning AI radar was similar to the majority of the Soviet fighters then in service. Initial sorties were set up so that the Lightning completed a standard intercept against a non-manoeuvring Buccaneer under controlled conditions. The aural indications proved the best way to initially identify the inbound fighter as a potential threat, while the strobe on the CRT made visual acquisition much easier. In a relatively short time, crews became adept at recognising the 'chirp-chirp' of the AI-23 radar carried by the 'Frightnings' and the standard strike progression tactics were modified to take advantage of the RWR.
>
> In those 'Dial a Lightning' days, many enjoyable sorties were flown. The standard profile involved two or four Buccaneers against two Lightnings and we set ourselves up about 100 nm east of Flamboro' Head. (It had to be something that the fighter pilots might recognise.) Once established at low level, the game was on. The fighters would set up a CAP [Combat Air Patrol] just to the east of Flamboro'. Our aim was to get to the end point without loss as the fighters tried to prevent this. As soon as a possible threat was identified, the formation would turn to increase the angle-off, thus presenting the fighter with a crossing target. (The range advantage offered by the RWR often meant that the fighter had not yet detected the target). In this way, we attempted to skirt around the threat. In the event that the fighter did maintain contact, he would be forced to turn towards the formation and continue closing to visual range. Again, this would soon become clear, since the intensity of both the aural and visual indications would continue to increase. If the fighter lost contact, the RWR indications would cease, and the strike would regain track. If contact was maintained, the intercept invariably became a stern chase, with the Buccaneers accelerating to 580 knots and 'going ultra-low', when the Lightning's impressive overtake capability usually proved inversely proportional to its fuel capacity! Once visual contact was made, standard evasion tactics were employed to defeat the air threat and maintain the attack track.
>
> The next stage of training substituted F-4s for the Lightning. Until the RWR, the F-4 enjoyed all the advantages. The pulse-Doppler radar gave them the ability to fire from beyond visual range (BVR). Of course, this is not as much fun as turning and burning, so they always closed-in for an AIM-9 or guns shot as well. The characteristics of the F-4 radar in search mode meant that it was not possible to assess the range or bearing of the fighter from any RWR indications. However, the F-4 also had no direct range information in search mode. They had to 'lock-on' in order to get an accurate range before firing and the RWR then indicated from which quadrant the lock-on CW emissions were being received. A turn through 90° away from the threat took us into the 'Doppler notch', at which point, their radar lock was broken and a BVR shot was ruined, so the fighter returned to search mode and tried again, or else closed to visual range for an AIM-9 or gun attack. These modes provided both visual and aural indications, and the threat was countered as for the Lightning.
>
> In summary, I believe the introduction of the RWR was probably the best thing to happen to the Buccaneer since its entry to RAF service. Crews were able to detect, and counter, air and surface radar threats so that evasive routeing could be initiated, so avoiding any threat engagement. The ready availability of Lightning and F-4 as air opponents, combined with the excellent facilities offered by Royal Navy ships provided exceptional training for Buccaneer crews.

During its final two years before decommissioning, 809 Squadron alternated between Honington and embarked periods on HMS *Ark Royal*. An examination of the squadron diary highlights a bewildering number of ports and airfields visited from Rio de Janeiro to Norway and the Caribbean to the Mediterranean and participation in many maritime exercises. Martel missiles were fired and countless bombs were dropped, including the 540-lb HE bomb, which was carried on a tandem beam. During exercises in the Baltic, tactics were devised to attack fast patrol boats with 2-in rockets fired under Lepus flares. An increasing number of RAF aircrew supplemented the Navy pilots and observers and they were to provide a valuable addition to the RAF squadrons in due course. A notable visitor to the Squadron was HRH The Prince of Wales, who arrived on board HMS *Ark Royal* on 21 September 1977 in the back seat of XV 869, with the Commanding Officer, Lieutenant-Commander Tony Morton, piloting the aircraft. After spending a few hours observing operations from the deck he was launched from the waist catapult and, after a low-level pass of the ship's port side, he returned to Yeovilton.

On 23 February 1978 the last Royal Navy pilot to be trained on the Buccaneer, Lieutenant Scott Lidbetter, (now a Rear Admiral), carried out DLPs on HMS *Ark Royal* in a 237 OCU aircraft, and a few days later he became the last pilot to join the Squadron. A few weeks later the Squadron left RAF Honington for the last time and embarked for a final six-month cruise and sailed for the weapon ranges off Puerto Rico and Florida. They also 'embarked' the RAF

The introduction of modern electronic warfare equipment in the mid-1970s increased the Buccaneer's survivability dramatically and had a major influence on tactics. The radar warning receiver aerials were housed in the front and rear bullets at the top of the fin, and the Westinghouse ALQ 101-8 ECM pod was carried on the outer pylon. Both systems were improved in later years. In this photograph the 237 OCU aircraft has the upgraded 101-10 ECM pod. (*Bob Poots*)

Honington Officers' Mess piano, thanks to the efforts of Rick Phillips and Tony Ogilvy, who later forwarded a modest cheque to the President of the Mess Committee at Honington by way of compensation. Once on board, the piano had to be dismantled in order to transfer it via numerous ladders and hatches to the Wardroom, where it was reassembled. Not surprisingly, even the efforts of a professional piano tuner failed to reproduce the correct noises, but it provided endless entertainment for a few months. Eventually, following the final aircraft launch in November, it was consigned to the deep by the steam catapult, with Captain Ted Anson acting as the FDO.

After participating in numerous exercises off the east coast of America, HMS *Ark Royal* sailed for northern waters to take part in Exercise 'Northern Wedding' and 809 Squadron found plenty of non-exercise trade with the Soviet Navy, in addition to flying long-range probes, ship attacks and close air support sorties. It was then time to sail to the Mediterranean for the final exercises. Port visits were made to Gibraltar, Naples and Athens, and on 4 November 1978 the Squadron said a formal farewell to the carrier with a 'Diamond Nine' led by the Commanding Officer. The final 809 Naval Air Squadron dinner was held on board on 17 November, when the Squadron gave its thanks to HMS *Ark Royal* for the help given and the comradeship established over the previous eight years.

One of the last visits for the ship was to Malta, and as HMS *Ark Royal* steamed out of one of the greatest ports ever used by the Royal Navy, over 10,000 local people lined the walls to bid farewell to the great ship as she quietly slipped her moorings in Grand Harbour with the paying-off pennant steaming behind in the wind. After a two-day flying period exercising with HMS *Galatea* and a short visit to Palma, it was time for the aircraft to leave the Royal Navy's last fixed-wing aircraft-carrier for the final time, and HMS *Ark Royal* steamed to a position near Majorca to

Buccaneers of 809 Squadron start engines ready to taxi forward to the catapult as HMS *Ark Royal* begins to turn into wind. (*Norman Roberson*)

With its 45-ft paying-off pennant streaming in the wind, and dressed overall with the Air Group in a ceremonial range, HMS *Ark Royal* bids farewell to Gibraltar for the last time on 2 October 1978. (*Ed Wyer*)

launch her Air Wing. On 27 November 1978 all the carrier's aircraft were prepared for launching despite the 'Mistral' wind blowing in excess of 40 kts and an associated rough sea. The Buccaneers of 809 Squadron launched after the Gannets and before the Phantoms of 892 Squadron, but one Buccaneer became unserviceable and was unable to launch until all other aircraft had departed. So it happened that Flight Lieutenant Rick Phillips and his Royal Navy observer, Lieutenant-Commander Ken MacKenzie, flying Buccaneer XV 863 had the honour of being the last aircrew to be catapulted from a British aircraft-carrier. It was also fitting that the Captain of HMS *Ark Royal* witnessing this unique piece of Royal Navy history should be 'Mr Buccaneer' himself, Captain Ted Anson, who had just been informed that he was to be promoted to Rear Admiral. Launching in one of the last Buccaneers was David Thompson, who had joined his first Buccaneer squadron fourteen years earlier and had accumulated over 2,000 hours on the aircraft in the meantime and risen to be the Senior Observer of the Squadron. He sums up his feelings after his final flight:

> It is difficult to pick out a single reason why the Buccaneer has become such an admired aircraft, which has retained the affection of all who flew it. It was built to do the business and looked as if it could and it was one of the few aircraft that the Royal Navy procured that was tailor-made for the job. It could go very fast and stay ultra-low, carry a lot and go a long way. The multitude of roles was another reason we all liked flying the aircraft and it was endlessly adaptable and never boring. The fact that it had two seats, with the never-ending banter between front and back, and two heads were certainly better than one. The way that the RAF aircrew took to the aircraft and to life on board cemented long-lasting friendships and respect. Although the Buccaneer never tossed a 'store' in anger, it did superbly well with the laser-guided bomb in the Gulf War. Now I look around my office and at the walls covered in Buccaneer photographs and pictures, it makes me feel great to have been a part of it.

The 809 Squadron aircraft were delivered to RAF St Athan, and soon afterwards the RAF formed another maritime squadron on 1 July 1979 at Honington, 216 Squadron commanded by Wing Commander Peter Sturt. The Pave Spike laser designator pod and the Paveway adaptor for fitment to the 1,000-lb bomb had been acquired for the RAF during 1979, giving the RAF its first laser-guided bomb capability. The Squadron was completing its operational work-up when the Buccaneer fleet was grounded following a fatal crash in Nevada. In due course there were insufficient aircraft to keep 216 Squadron in existence and 12 Squadron absorbed it on 4 August 1980, shortly after moving from Honington to Lossiemouth.

In near gale-force winds, the Buccaneers of 809 Squadron were launched from HMS *Ark Royal* for the last time on 27 November 1978. Before climbing away, they flew past in salute and departed to deliver their aircraft for continued service with the Royal Air Force. (*Terry Cooke*)

CHAPTER 7

Overland Operations

After working up for four months at Honington, XV Squadron moved in January 1971 to its permanent base at Laarbruch on the Dutch/German border, where it provided a major enhancement to the Commander Second Allied Tactical Air Forces (COMTWOATAF) order of battle. This was at the height of the Cold War, and the Squadron's first priority was to achieve a strike (nuclear) capability in order to take over the Quick Reaction Alert (QRA) commitment from the ageing Canberra force. The WE 177 nuclear store had recently been introduced to RAF service and the Buccaneer was configured to carry two of these weapons in the bomb bay. The density and capability of the air defence systems in Eastern Europe dictated that the Buccaneers would have to attack from low level and, with a short distance to the East German border, the Laarbruch-based Buccaneers remained low from take-off. Flight Lieutenant Dave Ray was one of the original XV Squadron pilots and he describes the early days at Laarbruch:

> The work-up for the strike role was mainly carried out as single aircraft flying day, low-level navigation sorties around the 2 and 4 ATAF areas. At the time,

The new-build aircraft for the RAF were initially assigned to the RAF Germany squadrons. Being refuelled in a dispersal at Laarbruch is XW 526, the first to equip XV Squadron. (*MAP*)

> the RAF Germany low-flying system was similar to that in the UK, with low flying areas connected by corridors or 'link routes'. We were able to fly down to 250 ft above ground level in this system and, once we left, we had to climb to 500 ft. There was no booking or control arrangements and, on a good day, we would see lots of other NATO aircraft, but only the Dutch seemed to be down at 250 ft with us. The weather in north Germany was often marginal, but we would fly whenever we could do so safely and get some benefit. A lot of the 2 ATAF area was covered by the North German Plain, which was very flat, and relatively featureless, presenting quite a challenge to the crews relying almost exclusively on visual navigation in those early days.

Tragedy struck XV Squadron two months after its arrival at Laarbruch when the Squadron Commander, Wing Commander David Collins, and his navigator, Flight Lieutenant Paul Kelly, were killed in XW 532. The aircraft entered low cloud just after take-off and crashed a few minutes later. This was a devastating blow for the newly formed squadron, but the arrival of Wing Commander Roy Watson as the new CO soon restored the morale of the Squadron. Roy Watson had recently completed a successful tour as the first Wing Commander Operations at Honington and had flown the Buccaneer. He had a fighter ground-attack background and was a very popular Squadron Commander. The Squadron went from strength to strength under his caring approach and leadership. His first priority was to complete the strike work-up programme to meet the NATO requirement.

Strike weapons were delivered from a toss profile or a laydown attack when a parachute-retarded weapon was used. Many overland targets were not radar discreet, so a 'vari-toss' profile, developed on a QWI Course, was used. This was a manual variation of the long-toss attack. The aircraft ran in at low level from an IP to a pull-up point and the bomb was released automatically by timer with the Buccaneer approaching a 60° nose-up attitude, when the pilot completed the standard toss recovery manoeuvre to escape at low level. Weapons training in the work-up to strike qualification was carried out at the RAF's own range at Nordhorn and on the Dutch coastal ranges at Vliehors and Terschelling. Nordhorn range was used so frequently that crews can still remember every detail, almost thirty years later. Flight Lieutenant Peter Eustace was one of the first navigators to join the second RAF Germany Buccaneer squadron, 16 Squadron, and he takes us down the bombing run on a laydown attack:

> To simulate a strike sortie we flew at 250 ft and 420 kts over the flat and often featureless North German Plain before turning towards the Kusten Canal and the junction with the River Ems, where we turned for the church at Rutenbrock. Over the church we set heading on 175° and started the stopwatch. The pilot flew at 200 ft on the radio altimeter and we had our first track check at the bend in the canal after twenty seconds. Rather than map read down the route, we waited for key check points to arrive at set times and then made appropriate heading changes. After ninety seconds, speed was increased to 500 kts and we looked ahead to pick up a row of four houses in the open and we flew by the fourth. We completed the weapons switches and looked for electricity pylons coming in from the left, and passed just to the left of where they crossed the road before looking for the final check, a junction of five minor roads known as the 'crow's foot' then passed the wind pump on the left and into the range area when I made the final weapon switch for a 'live' drop. The pull-up point for a dive attack came a few seconds later, but we pressed on to the circular strike target for a laydown attack. After the release of the weapon, switches were made safe as we carried out the escape manoeuvre. While most of us could have recited the run in our sleep, it was always stressful doing it for real as no two runs were the same.

Practice bombs were dropped from a special container, the carrier bomb light store (CBLS) in the bomb bay and the weapon selection

Opposite: The detailed map used by navigators as they approached the final stages of the attack run to drop a practice bomb on the strike target at Nordhorn range. (*Peter Eustace*)

procedures were the same as for a nuclear store; although crews became very familiar with the range and operational realism was lost, an attack at Nordhorn did allow timing techniques and the complex strike release procedures to be practised. Whenever possible, first-run attacks on other weapon ranges were carried out when more realistic bomb scores were achieved.

After meeting all the mandatory NATO requirements and criteria, XV Squadron was declared 'strike capable' with nuclear weapons from 1 July 1971. Following a few months in the wake of XV Squadron was 16 Squadron, which followed the same pattern of training and, once they were 'strike' declared, the two squadrons shared the QRA commitment for the next ten years. Flight Lieutenant Hilton Moses was among the first group of XV Squadron pilots to be declared 'combat ready' in the strike role, and he explains the QRA routine:

> Two crews and two aircraft armed with nuclear weapons were always at fifteen-minute readiness in the secure QRA compound; later we had hardened aircraft shelters. When we started a twenty-four hour QRA duty we first checked the weapon and 'cocked' the aircraft up to the point of engine start. We studied the allocated pre-planned target and kept ourselves amused and relaxed. Together with the ground crew and the RAF police guards, we ate and slept in the compound although we slept with most of our flying kit on in order that we could be taxiing the aircraft seven or eight minutes after the 'hooter' sounded. We practised the routine regularly but never started the engines in case a genuine call came, but we were able to make the practice more realistic once a fortnight. After two weeks, one of the aircraft was removed from the compound for routine servicing and a third was brought in with a new crew, loaded with a weapon and prepared for QRA. The weapon on the original aircraft was downloaded and then it was brought back to a ready status, minus a bomb. The alert would sound and all three crews reacted but only the outgoing crew started engines and they went through the full release procedures, taxied and took off on a simulated sortie to drop a bomb. After landing they recovered to the Squadron where the aircraft was

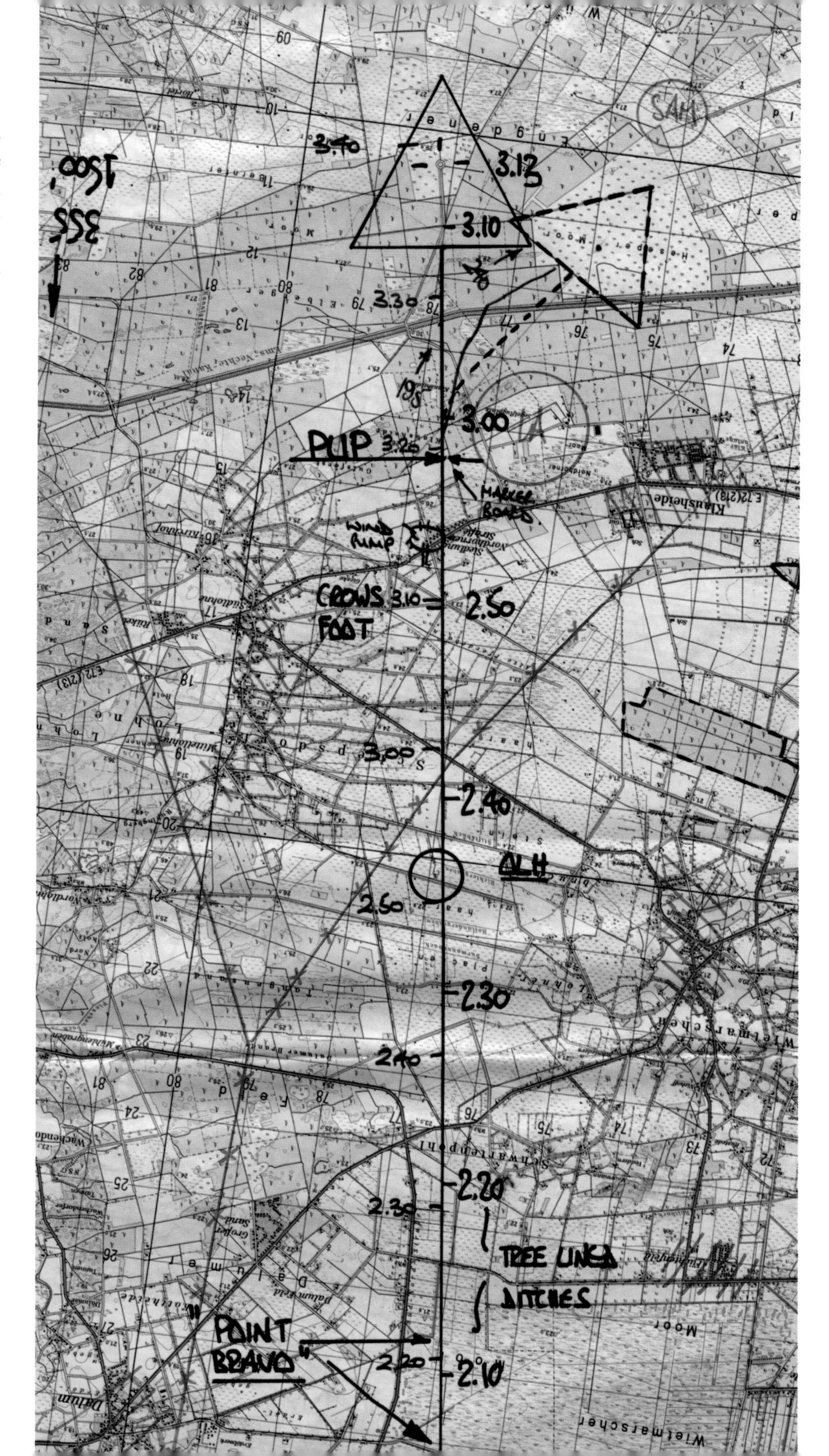

Buccaneers became a regular sight at low level over the North German Plain. This XV Squadron aircraft is in the wrap-around camouflage scheme introduced in the late 1970s and carries a CBLS, with practice bombs, on both outer pylons. (*Dick Cullingworth*)

> serviced and returned to routine flying. QRA was an evil necessity but, as my Station Commander once reminded me, it was why we were in Germany and I once calculated that I had spent twelve months of my life in the QRA compound. The price for winning the Cold War!

Declaration to NATO in the strike role was the priority for both squadrons, but they did not neglect the development of tactics and weapon delivery profiles for the attack role. They adapted for overland operations the profiles developed by the Royal Navy squadrons, and by 12 Squadron. Dave Ray explains the delivery modes used by XV Squadron in the early days of developing an attack capability:

> Initially, our weaponry was limited to dive-bombing with the 28-lb practice bomb in both the manual and automatic depressed sight line (MDSL & ADSL) modes. In MDSL, the pilot tracked the target in a 20° dive with the strike-sight aiming mark appropriately depressed, and deflected left or right to take account of the wind and any target movement, releasing the bomb on the navigator's height call at 2,000 ft. ADSL was similar, but the release computer released the bomb automatically when the calculated 'g' loading figure on the aircraft was reached as the pilot had to gradually reduce the loading on the aircraft to track the depressed sight line. This could be very accurate, but any wind or turbulence could create large errors, and the method soon fell into disuse in the overland role. In those early days, we also had 2-in rockets (replaced later with SNEB) fired in a 10° dive. It was nice to have a weapon that seemed to go where you pointed it, and arrived at the target before you flew over it! Later, we received the 4-lb practice bomb used to simulate the 1,000-lb retard bomb and we developed a shallow-dive attack with this retard bomb. This could be a very accurate attack when the crew got all the parameters correct.

During the Second World War, Lady MacRobert donated a Stirling bomber to XV Squadron in memory of her three sons killed flying in the RAF. The Squadron has maintained the tradition ever since. XT 287 carries the family crest by the roundel as it flies over a typical Rhineland scene. (*MOD/Crown Copyright*)

A 16 Squadron aircraft taxies from its Hardened Aircraft Shelter at Laarbruch. The Squadron markings are clear with the famous 'Saint' insignia displayed on the fin. The standard fit for RAF Germany-based Buccaneers did not include the air-to-air refuelling probe. (*Denis Calvert*)

The Buccaneer did not have a good navigation suite, and the need to launch a QRA aircraft could occur at any time of the day or night and in any weather. A Decca Doppler navigator, a twin gyro platform, the Ferranti Blue Parrot radar and a Tacan were the heart of the navigation system. This was the original fit of the Buccaneer Mark 1 for a maritime-only task when it had entered service with the Fleet Air Arm in the mid-1960s. The Decca Doppler was originally designed to work with a moving map display but the equipment fell out of favour with the Navy squadrons as Doppler soon proved to be unreliable over the sea. The twin-gyro platform produced a reasonably accurate heading output but had none of the sophistication or accuracy of an inertial navigation system. The Blue Parrot radar was a powerful I-Band radar with a 3° beam width based on the AI-23 air-to-air radar developed for the Lightning. After much trials development work on a variety of aircraft, including the Canberra, a number of changes were made to the production radar, including modifications to the pulse repetition frequency (PRF) and the pulse length to make the radar more suitable as a long range anti-ship radar. It proved to be very effective at finding ships in the middle of an uncluttered ocean, but the radar engineers at Ferranti never visualised the radar being used overland as a ground-mapping radar, and so the primary navigation aids for XV Squadron's crews were a comprehensively marked half-million topographical map, a reliable stop watch and a one-in-fifty-thousand map for target runs. The crew worked in very close harmony with each other, with the navigator reading from his map to the ground, pointing out relevant ground features to the pilot and asking him to confirm visual contact. The Tacan was a line-of-sight aid and therefore very limited in the low-level role. Until improvements could be made to the radar, aircraft were forced to fly a few hundred feet above the highest obstacle on the route, and this would have made the aircraft very vulnerable to the constantly improving air defence systems of the Warsaw Pact. Many thought that the likelihood of success for a strike aircraft flying at night or in poor weather was minimal.

Efforts were made to modify the Blue Parrot radar to give it a better performance overland, and a modification, called Monopulse Resolution Enhancement (MRE), was introduced in the early 1970s and a modest improvement was achieved. One of those most closely involved in perfecting new navigation techniques with the radar was Flight Lieutenant Tom Bradley, a navigator on XV Squadron who had also completed an exchange tour flying the with the Royal Navy:

> In August 1971 a team from CTTO came to the Squadron to organise low-level radar trials with the aim of determining whether the aircraft could legitimately be assigned a night capability. CTTO's plan was to fly a series of low-level sorties during the day, simulating night-flying conditions, with the navigator using radar predictions to assist his navigation. These predictions were meant to show a picture of what the navigator could expect to see 'painted' by the Blue Parrot radar and he could then compare and identify his present position. The pictures, it was claimed, would give a faithful representation of the radar 'paint' along a specific track at a specific height. Any other track or height would nullify the worth of the prediction. To collect data on the trials the navigator was tasked with taking pictures of the radar at specific geographic features for post-flight analysis. Unfortunately for the navigator, the only place to fit a camera was to wedge it into the radar visor, a frangible device, which protruded out from the radar over the navigator's knee. This was an obvious flight safety hazard for the navigator should he have to eject, when the heavy camera would strike his knee and, at best, cripple him for life. But CTTO had a solution. If the ejection was premeditated, all the navigator had to do was remove the camera and stow it away safely! Over a three-day period, ten sorties were flown at 500 ft and 420 kts, each lasting approximately ninety minutes in duration. The routes chosen were mainly to the east of Laarbruch, across the Rhine to the Osnabruck Ridge and then north over the North German Plain, before returning to the airfield for an internally-directed radar approach. To

The Buccaneers of XV and 16 Squadrons provided RAF Germany's tactical nuclear capability for thirteen years. This XV Squadron aircraft is over-flying the Moehne Dam. (*Author's collection*)

> everyone's great surprise, particularly the navigator's, the results were much better than expected, particularly over the more hilly terrain. As the trial progressed it also became apparent that the Blue Parrot 'painted' quite well certain cultural features like canals and towns, which were not shown on the radar predictions, and this added to everyone's confidence that maybe the aircraft had a reasonable capability at night after all. The photographs taken during the flights supported this view.

However, the navigation deficiencies in the overland role were not just limited to the radar. The Blue Jacket Doppler produced a reasonable groundspeed output, but it was of very limited use otherwise. In an attempt to overcome this, a modification to the navigation system was introduced in the 1970s. Known as the Ground Position Indicator Connector (GPIC) Unit, this was an interface between the radar, the Doppler and the air data computer designed to give the navigator an accurate positioning and waypoint system to enable him to accurately plot his position overland with a high level of accuracy. Trials results were very promising, but, unfortunately, the system did not fully live up to expectations in service as it was reliant on the unreliable accuracy of the overall Buccaneer navigation system, but it did provide a worthwhile improvement. Following the radar trial and the introduction of the GPIC, the Buccaneer was considered to have a night

The two-seat Hunter was used for pilot proficiency check sorties and instrument ratings. It was also used to provide a fighter 'bounce' against Buccaneer formations. WV 318 was a former F-4 variant converted to a T 7 standard and is carrying four overload fuel tanks to increase low-level range. The aircraft was bought by a private syndicate in 1995 and is a regular performer on the UK air shows circuit. (*MOD/Crown Copyright*)

capability and could therefore meet its NATO obligations. Subsequent Taceval results seemed to support this, and night flying using the Blue Parrot and GPIC became an accepted way of life for the RAF Germany Squadrons. The Headquarters air staff required each crew to carry out a certain amount of night flying each month, and this included navigation using the radar map predictions and radar bombing with the upgraded Blue Parrot. Although the terrain was ideal, achieving an operational capability was neither easy nor realistic, since all the town lights were on and the noise abatement lobbies limited the heights and routes that could be flown. The standard night route consisted of flying around north Germany at 2,000 ft and 420 kts and passing through the electronic warfare range at Borgholzhausen, before dropping a smoke-and-flash practice bomb at Nordhorn range, then returning to Laarbruch. The route became familiar to all Buccaneer crews as a 'Night Charlie'. Flight Lieutenant Bob Poots of XV Squadron remembers his first such sortie:

> During the afternoon I planned the sortie based on a precise time-on-target at Nordhorn. Working backwards from this time I worked out when to be at turning points, ending with a time for take-off. At the appointed hour, my pilot, Flight Lieutenant Rick Pierson, and I climbed into our flying kit, signed for the aircraft and headed out in to a wet and wild night. After checking the aircraft and a careful inspection of the ejection seat, we strapped in and completed the mass of checks and taxied out. As soon as we were airborne we ran into scudding cloud and 'stair-rods' of rain, so I buried my head in the left corner of the cockpit looking at the radar trying to identify the first turning point. In the subdued red cockpit lighting I checked the route book for the radar prediction, but it looked nothing like the radar picture! I checked the stopwatch, which agreed roughly with the GPI, and set course for the next turning point, which did appear looking like the prediction. Controlling my surprise, I identified the Borgholzhausen range by using the RWR and identifying the ground radar that had 'locked up' to us. I grabbed the weapon checklist for the run

> through the range, where we simulated dropping a bomb by transmitting a tone at the release point.
>
> We turned north in the rain and fifteen minutes later I identified the wide bay at Bremerhaven, updated the GPI and asked Rick for another 20 kts as we were behind the time line. Over the church at Leer we started to descend in cloud and turned on to the attack heading for the Nordhorn strike target and accelerated to 500 kts for a radar laydown attack. I placed the radar markers in the area of the target and identified the response from some electricity pylons, then picked up the target, moved the markers over it and checked the timing. At 8 miles, Rick descended to 400 ft when I took an even closer interest in the radio altimeter lights that I could monitor over his right shoulder. We broke cloud and called 'in hot' and were cleared, so I selected 'singles' on the bomb distributor and Rick squeezed the accept bar on cue and, after the pre-release timer had run down, the bomb dropped and we called clear and climbed back in to cloud and headed for Laarbruch.
>
> We landed after being airborne for just sixty minutes. The bomb was in the right place and the timing was OK, so it wasn't bad for a first effort. After the debrief we drove home together, back to the world of wives, babies and married quarters in the German town of Goch. Life in RAF Germany was full of contrasts!

The Buccaneer's long range and weapons load made an immense contribution to COMTWOATAF's attack capabilities. Both Laarbruch squadrons were tasked in the Offensive Counter Air (OCA), Battlefield Air Interdiction (BAI) and Close Air Support (CAS) roles. In the OCA role, the Buccaneers were tasked to attack airfields and enemy air defence positions, such as radar and missile sites. Against large static targets, such as airfields, the aim was to saturate the enemy air defences by coordinated attacks from different directions before sticks of six 1,000-lb bombs were tossed at the target. Lines of communication, including road and rail bridges, choke points and convoys, were the most likely targets in the BAI role, when the more accurate bunt retard or laydown mode was preferred. CAS operations were normally the preserve of the Harrier and Jaguar forces, but they offered a secondary role for the Buccaneer squadrons and, in the early days, they were practised with FACs of 1st (British) Corps. The most likely targets would have been concentrations of armour and mobile air-defence systems, when the most effective weapon was the BL 755 CBU delivered from a laydown attack. However, the principal attack option was OCA. This task had a high priority in the war plan and, to reduce reaction time, a number of missions were pre-planned. The primary Laarbruch mission was known as 'Option Alpha', which involved a six-ship coordinated attack on one of the high-value Warsaw Pact airfields in East Germany. Squadron Leader Bob O'Brien was a Flight Commander Operations on XV Squadron and he describes an Option Alpha war sortie:

> Our target was a large airfield, partly concealed in woods, with at least four aircraft dispersal sites. It was defended by a SAM 3 site and AAA defences. Our tactics were to send two aircraft ahead to carry out toss attacks against the SAM site with airburst 1,000-lb bombs, followed, thirty seconds later, by the main formation attacking the airfield using 1,000-lb retard bombs in the laydown mode. The pair

There is a full war load on this 16 Squadron Buccaneer, which is carrying full overload fuel capacity, a Westinghouse ALQ 101-8 ECM pod and a Paveway 1,000-lb laser guided bomb. Nestling in the open bomb bay are four 1,000-lb HE bombs. (*Terry Cooke*)

attacking the SAM site had the more difficult and vulnerable task, as they had to carry out a modified version of medium toss without the benefit of a radar lock-on, for which the weapon system had been designed. This was achieved by running in from a visual IP and pulling up at a set range from the target, relying on the weapons computer and a timer to release the bombs. The results were not always accurate and, for safety reasons, we could only practise this profile on the larger UK coastal weapons ranges. The four 'laydown' Buccaneers had separate attack tracks to achieve surprise. Their aiming points were aircraft in the dispersal areas or, if no aircraft were seen, hangars and static facilities. The main threats to the mission were AAA and enemy fighters, as we would be flying well below the engagement envelope of the SAMs available at that time. With the bomb door fuel tank in addition to external wing tanks, the target airfield was comfortably within range, so the formation could afford to transit at 480 kts from the time it crossed the border and to maintain 500 kts plus in the target area. We planned to fly at 250 ft initially and drop down to 150 ft as we came within radar detection range at the border, before letting down for the laydown attacks at 100 ft. The routes in and out had been planned to avoid known defences and, where our intelligence sources had failed to predict AAA, we hoped to negate weapon effectiveness by maximum use of terrain screening. The fighter threat was also a serious concern. Whilst at that time there was no credible look-down shoot-down missile capability, some of the later marks of MiG, in particular the MiG-21, could have caught us for a guns kill. Our tactics therefore relied upon impeccable lookout to gain an early sighting of any fighter, so that we could manoeuvre hard and fly lower to lose him or make his gun tracking very difficult. The last-ditch tactic of exploding a retard 1,000-lb bomb into the face of a fighter attempting to track from astern was also briefed. Had it ever been called, Option Alpha would have been an excellent test of the Buccaneer where it operated best; that is, fast and low!

During the annual evaluation of the station's war fighting capability conducted by the NATO Tactical Evaluation Team (Taceval), genuine war mission folders were made available: aircraft were bombed up with a war load and a full flight briefing conducted in front of the evaluation team. A simulated profile, involving a practice bomb run on Nordhorn range, followed by simulated attacks

In the offensive counter air role, Buccaneers approached and attacked the target at very low level and these tactics were practised regularly against NATO airfields. Squadron Leader Ken Tait of XV Squadron carries out a simulated airfield attack with bomb door open at Laarbruch. (*Peter Rolfe*)

The availability of former Royal Navy AIM 9-B Sidewinder air-to-air missiles in 1978 gave the RAF Germany Buccaneers a genuine self-defence capability for the first time. None were fired, but the carriage of them on training sorties sent a message to any potential adversary, and friendly fighters paid even greater respect during 'Dial a Lightning' fighter affiliation training sorties. (*Denis Calvert*)

against NATO airfields, was also planned and regularly flown. The evaluation team also checked the Squadron's ability to meet the standard NATO response time for generating a four-aircraft attack package, which was one hour. During Taceval, much blood, sweat and gamesmanship were expended in getting the ultimate 'Grade Ones' for Strike, Attack and Ability to Survive operations. Flight Lieutenant Malcolm Caygill was a navigator on 16 Squadron and he experienced many 'alert exercises' during his time on the Squadron:

> As we all came to realise, there was nothing like practice bleeding so Taceval was preceded by an RAF Germany alert exercise, a Maxeval and, since the Station Commander wanted to be sure everything was right, he ran a series of his own Minevals. They all followed the same pattern.
>
> Planning, preparing and briefing a four-ship attack sortie to the necessary standard and inside the required timescale took some organisation. The task was usually two SAPs with a specific time on target, followed by weapon drops on the range including a timed laydown bomb on Nordhorn. The lead crew obtained the intelligence and the task and they agreed the route split and rejoin points and the IPs for the SAPs. The lead pilot and his number three prepared the first set of target maps and confirmed the IP-to-target runs, while the two navigators planned the route, timing and attack profiles. Each crew member in the formation had to carry a half-million scale route map and a set of one-in-fifty-thousand scale target maps for each of the targets. Life was easy if the IP-to-target run was all on a single map but 'Sod's Law' often delivered the dreaded four-mapper when the planning room was a maelstrom of whirling craft knives, scissors, thirty-six large maps, plastic templates, felt-tip pens, tubes of rubber glue, coffee and bacon baps. Meanwhile, the number two crew was preparing the domestic and range brief and crew four copied any map that stayed still long enough. Anyone not involved in this fracas was roped in to accept the weapon load and prepare the aircraft. It was a relief to get airborne!

Attack tactics varied depending on the nature of the target. However, one could always depend on having to contend with a very hostile air defence system of radar-laid anti-aircraft artillery (AAA) and a wide variety of surface-to-air missiles (SAMs) layered from very low level to high level. To combat this most formidable threat the Buccaneer's basic tactic was to fly at ultra-low-level in a wide battle-formation, with aircraft up to 4,000 yds apart depending on the visibility. This gave the formation the maximum flexibility for manoeuvre in attack and defence and provided mutual support between aircraft and elements. Each member of the formation had a specific duty, with the leader's primary responsibility being the safe conduct and navigation of the formation. Number three was the deputy leader, with responsibility of monitoring the leader so that he could take over at any moment. He was also responsible for determining the correct position of the formation in relation to the leader and he supplemented the lookout. The job of the numbers two and four was 'to stick, to search, to report'. Good positioning was essential for good lookout and they were the eyes of the formation. The whole success of a sortie depended on the early sighting of all 'bogeys', and the Buccaneer cockpit provided both crew members with outstanding lookout. Whoever saw the threat first called the counter and controlled the action until the leader took over. The Buccaneer was in its element at 100 ft and it was a brave fighter pilot that attempted to get below to try for a guns kill.

The advent of the RWR gave the navigators an additional role as they could detect potential missile and fighter threats before they came into sight and counters could be called before the threat developed. Tactics against these visual and radar threats were practised regularly. Malcolm Caygill recalls typical exercises during his time on 16 Squadron:

> A service much appreciated by the frustrated fighter pilots on the Squadron was the 'Dial a Lightning' option. As the crews walked to their aircraft a quick call to Gutersloh Ops would usually guarantee a Lightning or two on CAP near the Coesfeld TV mast in Low Flying Area Two, ready for a spot of aggressive combat as the team crested the Osnabruck ridge where we tried to get rid of them by inverting and pulling down into the German Plain below. Mind you, by then he was probably out of fuel anyway!
>
> Having been entertained by Dave Wilby's lecture on the Wide-Band Homer during the OCU course, we at Laarbruch thought little more of EW [electronic warfare]. However, on days when the visibility dropped near to the legal limit for low flying, it was noticeable, that whilst adroit use of the radar stopped us bumping into the ground, it didn't stop us nearly hitting other folk who were stumbling their way through the murk as well. The arrival of the RWR changed all that and we could hear some of them. The majority of the passing trade was F-104s and Phantoms stooging around at 800 ft, with their radars blasting away so we could then avoid or menace them at will. However, that left the non-transmitting helicopters, Harriers, Jaguars, Mirages, G-91s and the occasional glider and airship to contend with. Germany was a busy airspace.

This is not a typical war load. The Buccaneer's spacious bomb bay was used for many purposes other than the carriage of bombs. Flight Lieutenant Hilton Moses, QFI and Entertainments Officer of XV Squadron, is supervising the loading of sixteen large demijohns of Kokineli wine at RAF Akrotiri in Cyprus prior to ferrying them back to Laarbruch for the annual cocktail party. (*Dave Herriot*)

Instructor crews of 237 OCU made regular sorties to Laarbruch to remain familiar with the overland tactics. This aircraft is parked in front of a first-generation NATO Hardened Aircraft Shelter (HAS) capable of housing one aircraft. (*Jell Sjoerdsma*)

> Perhaps the most sporting use of the RWR was during air defence exercises against the UK Air Defence region. The sorties from Germany entailed a low-level night-time dash across the North Sea, at high speed, to attack a target near the East coast. Whilst this was a scene where 12 and 809 Squadrons were in their element, it was challenging for the Laarbruch crews in the pitch black watching the RWR screen for the intercepting UK-based Phantoms to attack. We picked up their radar emissions then turned through ninety degrees to hide in his 'Doppler notch' then reverse to buster out [accelerate to high speed] to the target, staying too low for him to claim a valid Fox 1 or Fox 2 kill. Exciting stuff – and having to wear an immersion suit as well!

During the early 1970s NATO decided to implement an Airfield Survival Measures (ASM) programme. The dependence of modern air defence and strike/attack aircraft on long runways and complex support facilities made static airfields very vulnerable to air attack, and so a series of 'survive to operate' measures was implemented. This included the construction of dispersed Hardened Aircraft Shelters (HAS), hardened Pilot Briefing Facilities (PBF) and a custom-built Combined Operations Centre (COC). Each squadron had nine HAS and one PBF, usually dispersed at each corner of the airfield. It was soon recognised that the traditional organisation and practices for engineering and logistic support, in addition to the organisation of flying, had to change radically for operations in the 'hardened' era. Hilton Moses was on XV Squadron when the HAS era started, and he relates the new concept:

> The introduction of the HAS dictated a whole new way of operating. The original thought was to operate from the hangar in peacetime and move to the HAS in wartime, but we decided early on that we could not do one thing every day and expect to be proficient in war if we then switched to an unfamiliar system, so it was decided that we would operate from 'the hard' all the time. In other words, train for war in peace. Unfortunately, the principle was fine, but the additional support to operate efficiently was very slow to arrive and simple problems became a nightmare. Starting four aircraft from an apron required a few ground crew, a couple

Although in its element at very low level, the Buccaneer handled well below 10,000 ft, and a 'tail chase' of four aircraft during a strike progression (evasion) exercise often concluded a routine training sortie. This XV Squadron aircraft, flown by Flight Lieutenant Roger Sunderland, is pictured off the south coast of Cyprus during a detachment in 1978. (*Peter Rolfe*)

of electrical sets and two starters. Once we moved to the HAS, we needed one of everything – and a lot more ground crew. If one aircraft went unserviceable the crew could have quarter of a mile to travel to the spare aircraft in another HAS. Because of screening from buildings, we couldn't speak to each other on the radio and had to taxi forward. In time these problems were resolved, and it was definitely the way to operate. It was no good discovering the problems when the bombs started to drop.

The ASM programme dictated changes to other long-standing and well-proven methods of mounting flying operations. The RAF Germany airfields each had one long runway and there was always the possibility that it could be put out of action, leaving many aircraft serviceable on the ground but unable to take off. Minimum take-off distances were calculated so that aircraft could use a partly damaged runway and take off to fly to other airfields to be re-armed and refuelled for a war sortie. Crews also practised flying from the narrow parallel taxiway. Teams of Royal Engineers, expert in rapid runway repair, were attached to each airfield; the RAF Regiment provided airfield air defence with Rapier SAMs, and Field Squadrons patrolled the perimeter of the airfield to guard against saboteurs. All these complex measures were reasons for operating every day from the HAS complexes and the procedures were tested regularly, culminating in the annual Taceval

The pattern of flying in Germany varied little over the years. A steady stream of exercises on the Continent and over the United Kingdom, interspersed with training and exercise detachments, regular no-notice alert exercises and the constant requirement to mount QRA, provided the regular routine for the personnel of XV and 16 Squadrons.

The formation of 208 Squadron at Honington, in June 1974, introduced a new aspect of overland operations. The Squadron was assigned to the Northern Flank of NATO for operations in the Baltic region and throughout Norway. Tactics for operations in the Baltic Approaches

Armourers of XV Squadron prepare to load the final BL 755 Cluster Bomb Unit (CBU) into the bomb bay during a detachment to Cyprus. The BL 755 was the most likely weapon to be used against interdiction and close air support targets, such as armour and convoys. (*MOD/Crown Copyright*)

(BALTAP) were very similar to those used by the two RAF Germany squadrons. The terrain and the threat were also similar, but 208 had to operate over much longer ranges and they made regular use of air-to-air refuelling and regularly staged through airfields in Denmark. To practise procedures and acquaint the NATO air staff in the regional headquarters, the Squadron regularly deployed to RDAF airfields at Aalborg, Karup and Sykdstrup and participated in regional exercises. Low flying and weapon range facilities were limited in Denmark, so 208 Squadron were regular visitors to Laarbruch, where they enjoyed the support facilities of their sister squadrons, the wider variety of weapon ranges in Holland and Germany, the opportunities for low flying down to 250 ft – and the duty free!

Throughout the period of 208 Squadron's assignment to NATO in the overland role, it was always considered more likely that they would be required to reinforce the Allied Air Forces in Norway. This presented a very different challenge and tactics had to be modified considerably. The terrain and the weather were completely different from those in the Baltic region and the hours of daylight varied greatly throughout the year. Distances were prodigious, but the introduction of the bomb door fuel tank was a huge bonus. To provide maximum range, the Squadron always flew with wing tanks fitted, and many sorties included refuelling in Norway on both outbound and return legs. The threat was also considerably different. Unlike the Central Region of NATO, there were no massed area air defences, and the approaches to targets could often be made relatively safe by the masking of a low-level approach using the very rugged terrain thus allowing a much greater degree of surprise attack. However, individual targets were very heavily defended and the element of surprise was often the Buccaneers' only chance of survival until stand-off weapons were introduced. The Squadron practised coordinated attacks against airfields, in anticipation of being used in the

The terrain of Norway presented 208 Squadron with very different conditions for the overland role, but north Scotland provided some excellent training opportunities, and detachments to Lossiemouth were a regular feature of the Squadron's training programme. (*BAe Systems*)

offensive counter-air role, and it was in regular demand as the 'enemy' attacking RNoAF airfields, radar installations and SAM sites. There were very few roads in the northern regions of Norway and, armed with BL 755 cluster bombs, the Squadron was tasked with interdiction sorties to attack advancing armour or convoys. Another important (and difficult) role for 208 Squadron was to counter amphibious landings, but there were few opportunities to train for this specialised role.

During its earlier illustrious history, 208 Squadron had spent many years in Egypt; indeed, the centrepiece of the Squadron badge was a Sphinx. For its regular visits to the frozen north, the training sorties went under the apt description of 'Exercise Blue Sphinx', and there were few weeks when a pair of the Squadron's Buccaneers was not operating over Norway. Crews became very adept at operating from snow-covered runways, coping with 'white-out' conditions and making significant in-flight re-routeing plans to avoid bad weather and cloud-filled fjords. At other times, the visibility could be in excess of 100 miles with constant daylight. The only way to be effective in these greatly varying conditions was to practise frequently and 208 Squadron crews regularly participated in exercises over Norway, including operating from Norwegian airfields. During a Taceval exercise on 25 November 1980, Flight Lieutenant Eddie Wyer was the leader of a four-aircraft formation tasked to take off from Honington to attack a RNoAF airfield, drop some practice bombs on a weapons range and land at Oerland on the coast at the western end of the Trondheim Fjord:

> We took off in the dark at 6.00 a.m. and flew high level before descending off the southern coast of Norway to carry out a coordinated attack against the airfield at Lista. After the attack we formed up in wide battle formation and headed for the Telemark low-flying area, covered in snow and requiring very careful monitoring of the altimeter in the near white-out conditions. As the weather deteriorated, I abandoned the bombing detail on Hjerken weapons range and headed for Oerland.

The weather got worse and very heavy snow showers were over the airfield as we approached from the south. I sent the first pair ahead and they just landed on the snow-covered runway as the storm arrived and it was obvious that my number two and I had no chance. My regular navigator was the Boss; we had been together for eighteen months and both of us reached the same decision in the same instant. With limited fuel it was straight to the only other airfield in the region, the small airfield at Vaernes further inland up the fjord.

Our number two was the junior pilot on the Squadron, 'Boy' Southwood (later of ETPS fame) and he had never been to Norway before, let alone landed on snow. We had to race the weather and just made it as we broke into the circuit. The runway was the minimum length for a Buccaneer – in dry conditions! With no arresting gear, we had to employ maximum aerodynamic braking and just stopped in time, with very little fuel. We then had to taxi downhill and negotiate a tight corner to a very icy aircraft pan where we skidded to a halt. In doing so the airbrake hit the hangar door and the 'pen knib' on the end broke off. After shut-down we inspected the damage and I picked up the offending item when the Boss told me to 'shove it in my nav bag and I'll stick it back on when we return to Honington'. One of the advantages of flying with the CO! We checked that the Oerland pair had landed safely and went for a cup of tea and to convince 'The Boy' that it was all in a day's work on 208 and he would soon get used to it!

The sortie was far from over. After a few hours, the airfield was declared fit for take-off and the two aircraft taxied gingerly to the runway for take off with 'The Boy' holding on the taxiway to allow the snow to disperse as the leader rolled down a runway still covered in packed snow. The ensuing cloud of snow was spectacular and the number two followed the brief precisely, so rolled thirty seconds later despite the near zero visibility! Not a bad effort for a first visit to the snows – and no wonder he made a good test pilot in later life. The other pair had a similar experience taking off from Oerland, and the four-ship met up and flew back through Telemark before climbing out to return to Honington, landing in the dark. Flight Lieutenant Bob McLellan was one of the pilots leaving Oerland, and he recalls that there was still excitement to be faced:

> As we lined up on the runway at Oerland, a snow clearance vehicle was on the runway so the leader had to wait. He then took off in a cloud of snow and successfully got airborne. I waited until most of the debris thrown up by his aircraft had settled and then took off. We joined up with the pair from Vaernes and flew to our target before heading back to Honington. It was a very dark evening and we joined

The leader and his number two lift off. Most take-offs were unblown unless the runway was short or the aircraft was operating at maximum all-up weight. 208 Squadron made extensive use of air-to-air refuelling and the probe was a standard fit. (*BAe Systems*)

The steep fjords of Norway provided 208 Squadron with ample opportunities to use the terrain to mask the route and approach to targets, and so achieve surprise. Aircraft often flew as pairs down different fjords to meet up on the 'timeline' close to the target before attacking as a four-ship. (*BAe Systems*)

the circuit for a night visual pairs break thirty seconds behind the lead pair. Turning finals, two fireballs careering down the runway ahead of us greeted my nav and me. Both the tyres of my leader's aircraft had burst and he was rapidly demolishing the wheels on the runway. It was a very spectacular sight but our immediate concern was our fuel state, which had reached minimums so we immediately cleaned up the undercarriage and flaps and left for Wattisham, using minimum fuel and we just made it! It was the end of a very long fifteen-hour day and we still had to get back to Honington. It transpired that the leader had left the handbrake on whilst being distracted at Oerland and had got airborne with the wheels locked! Was it a testimony to the icy state of the runway, the ineffectiveness of the handbrake or the power of the mighty Spey engines?

The aircrew of 208 Squadron often took off in benign conditions at Honington and, 90 minutes later, were flying in extreme weather conditions in very rugged terrain. The far north of Norway presented unique conditions. A regular training sortie for a pair of aircraft was a high-level rendezvous with a Victor tanker off the east coast of Scotland, to refuel to full before descending to be low level 100 miles from the Norwegian coast. Flying in wide battle formation, the pilots were alert for RNoAF F-104 (later F-16) fighters, while the navigators monitored the RWR for the telltale sign of an air intercept (AI) radar. Once threatened, the Buccaneers countered by accelerating and staying very low as they set up a coordinated attack on the airfield at Oerland. With the attack completed, the aircraft flew low level up the Norwegian coast and crossed the Arctic Circle near Bod, where more fighters could be expected. The crews continued north using the high mountains to mask their approach as they prepared to drop practice bombs on the weapons range at Andoya in the north of the Lofoten Islands. After completing a laydown first-run attack, the pair returned to the nearby airfield to land, almost three hours after leaving Honington. The following morning an 'in-theatre' training sortie was flown and Eddie Wyer recalls a typical flight:

> After take-off on a blustery and cold morning we headed north at low level over the sea to cross the coast north of Tromso. The weather deteriorated and we had to work our way through the fjords in terrain that resembled the moon but eventually the lowering cloud base forced us back out to the coast where the sea was heaving. We flew round the North Cape, the most northerly part of Europe, and it was extremely forbidding country. A comment from the back seat, reminding me that at 200 ft we were out of radio contact with the world, made me concentrate even more on the engine instruments and fuel state. It was the most awful place to have to bale out should things have gone wrong. However, one could not help but find the whole place awe-inspiring. Eventually we reached the 25° east longitude, not far from the Soviet border, where the rules said we must turn back and we retraced our steps to Andoya. In the afternoon, it was another low-level flight to tangle with the Bod, F-16s before climbing out to return to the UK. As we coasted in over the lush, green countryside of Norfolk, it was difficult to visualise the contrast of a few hours earlier. Flying a Buccaneer on 208 was never dull.

The air and exercise staffs at Headquarters No. 1 Group were always seeking more effective training, and Exercise 'Provision' was one such exercise. With limited notice, the Squadron was required to generate four aircraft with a full conventional war load of up to six 1,000-lb inert bombs. This gave the armourers an excellent opportunity to practise their trade, and once the aircraft were loaded, the Buccaneers took off at maximum all-up weight. The exercise included air-to-air refuelling followed by transiting through a fighter CAP, mounted by Phantoms and Lightnings, before attacking two simulated targets. The four Buccaneers then flew to Garvie weapons range in the north of Scotland where they dropped the 1,000-lb bombs. Flight Lieutenant Ron Trinder was the QWI on 208 Squadron, and he remembers the value of the exercise:

> The exercise was considered to be the most realistic ever and we wanted more of the same type. With a load of 1,000-lb bombs and maximum fuel, we were able to fly at full combat weights allowing us to simulate war conditions. We certainly noticed the

Flying in the north of Norway provided some breathtaking flying, but a constant eye on the weather was essential. With so few airfields in the region, adequate fuel had to be retained for diversions. The terrain was forbidding and aircrews were trained in survival techniques should they have the misfortune to have to eject. (*Author*)

During most sorties flown by 208 Squadron, the aircrew arranged for Phantom CAPs to be positioned along their route, and both sides learnt many lessons. Unlike the crews of these 111 Squadron aircraft, few Phantom aircrews discovered what a Buccaneer looked like! (*Denis Calvert*)

> different handling characteristics at these high weights, whether we were on the tanker at 25,000 ft or flying in the steep valleys and evading fighters at very low level. The fighter CAPs were aggressive and persistent and, after landing, we were all interested to read a signal from 43 (F) Squadron, one of the opposing Phantom squadrons, which read, 'It is suggested that the Buccaneers carry realistic war loads in future or suffer the imposition of operating restrictions to simulate them.' Just how realistic did they want us to be?

To combat the formidable Warsaw Pact air defences, the RAF had adopted tactics built around the fast, low-level penetration of enemy airspace, and training for the Buccaneer overland squadrons was geared to this fundamental tactical philosophy. Unfortunately, in peacetime, such training conflicted with the need to adhere to air traffic procedures, to avoid built-up areas and to limit noise and pay attention to the increasingly vociferous voice of the environmental lobby.

All these factors had a considerable influence on training, and the problem was particularly difficult for the Germany-based squadrons, although it was not so acute in the United Kingdom. However, training for the major elements that underpinned tactical doctrine suffered from some severe limitations. Low flying had to be conducted in specified areas, which became very familiar to the crews, almost all the weapons ranges were situated on the coast with unrepresentative targets and fighter affiliation exercises had to take place over the sea. Electronic warfare was seen by many as a 'black art' and was little understood by the staffs. Of greater significance, there were virtually no training facilities for using and developing this significant and crucial capability, and squadrons were rarely able to practise tactics in a realistic EW environment. Collectively, these limitations created a situation in which realistic operational training was extremely difficult, and much of the training could only be classed as 'academic' although flying was tremendously exhilarating and demanding. The commencement, in May 1977, of detachments to Goose Bay in eastern

Canada, to spend a month conducting intensive low-flying training over the featureless forests and lakes of Labrador, was excellent value, but there were very few opportunities to train for the wartime role and the facilities available for operational training against realistic, simulated threats were extremely limited.

Prospects for an improvement in the attitude to operational training came from an unexpected but valuable source. During the mid-1970s the United States armed forces conducted a study to address the lessons learned from the Vietnam War. These studies had demonstrated that 'unseasoned' combat aircrews suffered unacceptably high loss rates whilst showing low operational effectiveness. Indeed, the first ten missions were the key to a crew's survival in war. This should not have come as a surprise since Luftwaffe General Adolph Galland had written in his Second World War memoirs: 'A steadily increasing percentage of the young inexperienced pilots were shot down before they reached their tenth operational flight. As training courses in the Luftwaffe were cut it soon became more than fifty per cent.'

The USAF decided to provide an operational training facility, which could reproduce those early war sorties, and in 1975 Exercise Red Flag was born at Nellis Air Force Base near Las Vegas in the Nevada desert. The tactical weapons and electronic warfare ranges to the north occupied an area that would cover the southern half of England and Wales, and they included fifty different types of life-size targets against which aircraft were allowed to deliver live weapons from any direction using any delivery mode. Targets included a battlefront, formed with 220 replicas of Soviet tanks deployed in realistic formations, and there were two truck convoys – one of them, no less than 17 miles long – spaced in exactly the same way as a Soviet convoy. Airfields had been scraped out of the Nevada desert to the exact pattern of those located in Eastern Europe and aircraft were parked in dispersal areas. Dummy and real missile sites had been constructed. There was

In 1977 Buccaneers of 208 Squadron deployed to Goose Bay in Labrador for a concentrated period of 100-ft low-level training over the huge expanse of featureless forests and lakes. The wrap-around disruptive camouflage proved very effective. Such detachments became a regular feature for all RAF fast-jet squadrons. (*Author*)

The pilot of this 208 Squadron Buccaneer has the undercarriage retracting almost before the aircraft is airborne. The speed of retraction was amazingly quick and was designed with carrier take-offs in mind. (*Jelle Sjoerdsma*)

even an industrial complex with rail access, complete with a train.

Visiting squadrons formed the attacking 'Blue' force and were opposed by the 'Red' forces, comprising many different SAM and AAA systems built to simulate the main threats posed by the Warsaw Pact forces. These included most of the Soviet systems, and only the missiles and bullets were missing from the simulations, but through the medium of video-camera recorders, many aircraft were 'shot down' by SAMs and 23-mm and 57-mm AAA. The final threats posed by the Red forces were the air defence fighters, controlled by a Soviet-style Ground Control Interception (GCI) network. A special squadron of 'Aggressors' was established and permanently assigned to Red Flag. Other USAF combat fighters supplemented them and gun-sight film was used to assess 'kills'. Crews who had a validated 'kill' against them from any threat became candidates for a combat survival scenario, the following day, on foot in the desert.

In early 1977, Tactical Air Command of the USAF invited the RAF to participate in a Red Flag exercise, and the air staffs decided to send ten Buccaneers and two Vulcans as the first non-US participants. As 208 Squadron was the only overland Buccaneer unit that practised air-to-air refuelling, it was decided that they would ferry their aircraft to and from Nellis. All 208 Squadron crews and four from 237 OCU participated in the first two-week period, and crews from XV and 16 Squadrons took over for the second period. Ten Buccaneers left Honington on 2 August 1977, in pairs, to rendezvous with Marham-based tankers en route to Goose Bay for an overnight stop, before taking off for Nellis the following day. After four days of acclimatisation, the exercise started.

Commanding the first RAF squadron to deploy for a Red Flag exercise was the Squadron Commander of 208 Squadron, Wing Commander Phil Pinney, who explains the flying programme:

Red Flag exercises began on a Sunday with briefings to cover the planned flying, the scenarios and the rules of combat. The plan was for each crew to fly eight sorties during the flying phase, which began the following day with EW orientation sorties and allowed us to listen to the threats on our RWR equipment and to test the effectiveness of our ALQ 101-8 ECM pods. On this sortie, the only one that was unopposed, we also took the opportunity to practise high-energy manoeuvring in the hot and high target area standing some 6–8,000 ft above sea level. To our delight, the Buccaneer performed admirably and we felt ready for battle.

On the remaining seven sorties for each crew we were opposed by the Red air and ground threats. At around midday, the Air Tasking Message for the following day's missions appeared. Our formation leaders then planned their coordinated attacks against the assigned targets and spent the rest of the day either de-conflicting or integrating with other Blue force units. This in itself proved to be a very valuable feature of the exercise, allowing crews to review their tactics in order to fit into a package of sorties rather than operating in isolation, which would never have been the case in a real conflict.

After take-off, the strike/attack forces penetrated 'enemy' airspace, frequently with sixty to seventy aircraft entering the target areas through a series of corridors within a period of 20 minutes. No radio calls were required and clearance to drop live weapons was automatic. Once in the range area, aircraft were constantly under threat from ground-based modern SAM systems, both real and simulated, and from the Aggressor squadron which was equipped with the F-5E fighter. These aircraft were chosen because they looked similar to a MiG-21 and they had comparable performance. To add to the realism, they were even camouflaged in the exact schemes of the Warsaw Pact, and their pilots, who spent a full three-year tour as an aggressor pilot, had been

For the first RAF participation in Exercise 'Red Flag' in August 1977, 208 Squadron tried a number of desert camouflage schemes. They were partially successful but few people could have visualised that something similar would be needed fourteen years later. Back at Honington, this aircraft is almost ready to start the port engine using the low-pressure air starter. (*Malcolm English*)

Two aircraft descend to low level in the desert range area. Comparisons between the camouflage schemes can be made. (*Terry Gazzard*)

indoctrinated and trained to copy and fly exactly as an enemy fighter pilot would. This allowed crews to fly the precise tactics that they would have employed in war, and they were not subconsciously devising tactics to counter the Phantom and Lightnings flown by their RAF colleagues – always a temptation when inter-squadron rivalry was at stake, but not representative of war.

The ground threats were extremely realistic and provided a unique opportunity to employ electronic warfare tactics and to use the ECM pod, something that was quite impossible during normal training in the UK. This exposure to the real world of electronic warfare was one of the most valuable aspects of the early Red Flag exercises. Not only did crews learn a great deal about tactics, but the opportunities also provided an excellent spin-off to assess the effectiveness of aircraft systems. Many modifications to aircraft and tactics stemmed from the experiences gained at Red Flag.

Ron Trinder was the 208 Squadron QWI and a formation leader on the first Red Flag. He describes a typical sortie:

> The basic tactic for the sortie was to route plan carefully and fly to obtain maximum terrain masking with minimum 'skylining' over ridges. We flew all the attack sorties in very loose tactical formations of two or four aircraft and we always aimed to keep crews as constituted pairs. This proved to be of tremendous value and we became almost telepathic and never once used the radio except to call a fighter threat. An increase in jet exhaust smoke or a change of heading denoted a threat, and an appropriate counter was thrown. We flew at 100 ft to the target using the radio altimeter, listening to the RWR and concentrating on terrain masking to remain undetected as long as possible whilst maintaining the 'timeline'. If threatened, we split to create multiple problems for the air and ground defences and joined up on the timeline as soon as possible, often as late as the target run. We soon discovered that our best defence in the face of an aircraft attack was to run. To turn was fatal. We also realized the need to avoid turning in the target area, as an aggressor aircraft would locate the bomb smoke and a turning aircraft was easier to spot than one which stayed low and kept on going. The lack of a self-defence weapon was our main problem, although we carried retard 1,000-lb bombs in the bomb bay – one dropped in front of a pursuing fighter proved a useful deterrent. I've yet to meet a fighter pilot that was prepared to carry on with an attack under such conditions.
>
> On each sortie we were able to drop live weapons from a first run attack. We had complete freedom to choose the mode and direction of attack, speed and release height and there was no range safety officer to baulk us at the last moment. Bombing with live high explosive bombs and cluster bombs provided another unique opportunity and crews had to be extremely precise in their timings to ensure that they did not fly into the real fragmentation debris created by the preceding aircraft. It was crucial that their weapon was dropped on time to ensure that the following aircraft was safe to attack. This required great discipline and skill, which could not possibly be replicated under the simulated conditions that prevailed during routine squadron training in the UK. We all know that aircrew like to 'claim' that they would have had a direct hit and been spot on time, but in Red Flag our results provided the proof

> of our claims or otherwise. Certainly, the level of traditional aircrew 'line-shooting' dropped significantly.

At the end of each day's flying came the mass debriefing, when some 300 exhilarated but exhausted aircrew assembled in one hall to recount the stories of their missions, tactics and results. This debriefing was the core of the Red Flag training programme, and many Buccaneer aircrew felt that this was the single, most valuable aspect of the exercise. It began with the day's Red Force air and ground claims being listed together with the umpires' assessment, and not surprisingly claims outnumbered validated 'kills' by about four to one. Each formation leader then gave an account of his mission before the Aggressors recounted their experiences. Phil Pinney summarises the feelings of all the Buccaneer aircrews that participated:

> The Red Flag staff conceded that our dedicated low-level tactics achieved results better than they had seen before. We watched the claims being listed at the first mass debriefing with apprehension but 'Buccaneer' did not appear. Our confidence grew each day as no 'kills' were registered against us and we knew that the ground threats had never faced an aircraft flown so consistently low and fast. The aggressors found the Buccaneer hard to acquire visually as they received no assistance from their Soviet-styled GCI network that never knew of our presence flying at 100 ft. As a result, they pulled in the F-15 Eagle with its look-down radar and the odd claims were validated. After a week we felt the full weight of the F-5 and F-15 patrols being thrown against us and we felt sorry for our colleagues on XV and 16 Squadrons who had to fly the second half of the exercise. They faced a 'MiG Alley' hornet's nest from their very first missions but they met the challenge.
>
> Without question, the Buccaneer crews came home from Red Flag knowing that, in the Buccaneer, we had one of the world's best operational strike/attack aircraft of its day. At Red

Aircrew drawn from the two RAF Germany squadrons completed the second phase of the first Exercise 'Red Flag' and pose here with the Detachment Commander, Group Captain John Walker, at the end of the highly successful RAF participation. Wing Commander Peter Oulton, the Officer Commanding XV Squadron, is on the Group Captain's right. (*Terry Gazzard*)

Before departing Nellis, the Buccaneers fly through the range area to say farewell . . . and to give the air defence and ground radar controllers their first sight of the mighty 'Banana' jet! (*Norman Browne*)

> Flag we flew it faster, further and lower when carrying more than any other participant. It possessed a good EW capability and with a two-man constituted crew we were able to penetrate the defences with gratifying success. We returned home confident that if we had to go to war, we could do so effectively. Red Flag was, for all of us, the most exhilarating, demanding and professionally satisfying flying we had ever experienced.

No Buccaneer aircrew that participated in Red Flag would disagree. The crews also made a significant impression on their USAF hosts, and Red Flag 77-9 became the forerunner of annual visits by all types of RAF strike/attack aircraft that continue to this day. The US Defense and Foreign Affairs Daily was clearly impressed and headlined the performance of the three Buccaneer squadrons:

> RAF Buccaneers have performed outstandingly well [at Red Flag]. The low-level performance of the aircraft has allowed RAF pilots [sic] to show off some of their tactics to USAF counterparts. Some of the tactics have been so 'sharp' that the USAF pilots in the F-5Es have been unable to cope with the Buccaneers at all. Close observers say that some of the tactics adopted by the Buccaneer crews have astounded the USAF who are surprised that an aircraft now some seventeen years old can defeat the efforts of such types as the F-5E and F-15 aggressors. To others it is no surprise. The Buccaneer has long been one of the most underrated aircraft in combat inventories. Its low-level performance has become legendary.

An immediate fallout of the Red Flag experience was the introduction of the 100-ft low-flying areas in Scotland and improvements to the Spadeadam EW range. The constant availability of Tain weapons range, the ever-present 'Dial a Phantom' force at Leuchars and dodgy weather provided an ideal arena for tactical overland training. Even the RAF Germany squadrons found excuses to mount regular detachments to Machrihanish, and Lossiemouth became a second home to all the Buccaneer squadrons. Scotland provided outstanding training options for tactical training and many Buccaneer aircrew claimed, justifiably, that the facilities were the best in Europe. Before embarking on future Flag exercises, each squadron spent two weeks completing a carefully programmed work-up period at Lossiemouth, culminating in an eight-ship coordinated attack at Tain range after penetrating the EW range and fighter CAPs without once flying above 100 ft. All aircrew acknowledged that there was a considerable difference in techniques when flying at 100 ft, as compared with the standard clearances of 250 ft, and Lossiemouth training detachments proved to be an ideal preparation for the major overseas exercises. In February 1980, the Officer Commanding 208 Squadron wrote:

> The operational training value of our work-up at Lossiemouth was exceptional. Both the terrain and the weather were typical of the conditions we encounter in the AFNORTH region. In the eight sorties flown by each crew, there is greater value obtained than in many times that number of sorties elsewhere.

The three overland squadrons paid regular visits to participate in Red Flag, but tragedy struck on 7 February 1980, the penultimate day of the third exercise. XV 345 suffered a catastrophic failure of the starboard wing as the aircraft breasted a ridge in the range area. Squadron Leader Ken Tait and his navigator, Flight Lieutenant Rusty Ruston, were killed, and the loss of this popular crew in such a catastrophic accident was a devastating blow to the close-knit Buccaneer community. The Buccaneer fleet was grounded pending investigations, which subsequently highlighted that the failure had occurred in the front spar of the inner wing. British Aerospace investigations at Brough found several reasons for this failure. The fatigue test airframe had been a Mark 1, which, in the event, proved less than relevant to the Mark 2 and the different profiles flown overland. All aircraft were inspected and those least affected were modified. After a prodigious amount of research and work by the British Aerospace engineers at Brough, some sixty aircraft were returned to service. Throughout the grounding, XV and 16 Squadrons maintained QRA at Laarbruch and the aircraft would have flown in the event of war, but by the end of July the grounding order was lifted and the squadrons commenced training. The priority in aircraft allocation was given to the RAF Germany squadrons and to 12 Squadron as the only maritime squadron. In the event more aircraft were recovered than originally anticipated and there were sufficient to equip 208 Squadron and 237 OCU, but the recently formed 216 Squadron ceased to exist as a Buccaneer unit. As an historical footnote to the five-month grounding of the UK's Buccaneer force, Headquarters No. 1 Group retrieved a number of Hunter FGA 6 and 6a aircraft on which squadron pilots could maintain a degree of flying currency. This was the

Following the great success of Exercise 'Red Flag' new 100-ft low-flying areas were opened up in Scotland and all future work-up training for similar exercises was conducted out of Lossiemouth. This 208 Squadron aircraft (displaying the 216 Squadron badge) approaches the Tain weapons range for a first-run attack with a 28-lb practice bomb, carried in a CBLS, on the laydown bombing target. (*Andrew Brookes*)

During the Lossiemouth work-up for Exercise 'Maple Flag' 1981, the navigator Squadron Commander of 208 Squadron (the author) completed his 100 hours flying time in the Hunter, and was inducted into the 'Hunter Mafia' by his three Flight Commanders, Squadron Leaders Terry Heyes, David Ainge and Rob Wright. They had a mere 5,100 Hunter hours between them! (*Author*)

first (and last) recorded example of a single-seat type appearing in the Group's inventory; and what better aircraft to claim that honour!

Red Flag continued to be a regular activity, and not all transits were made with the aid of the excellent tanker force. The Buccaneer had the most incredible range for a two-seat strike-attack aircraft, and in October 1981 the Buccaneers of 16 Squadron were tasked with self-ferrying (without AAR) aircraft to Nellis for yet another exercise, and this gave the Buccaneer the opportunity to demonstrate its capability. With full wing tanks, a full bomb door tank and a full bomb bay ferry tank (a total of 24,190 lb) the aircraft flew against the prevailing wind to North America via the Azores to Gander following the Great Circle route and then to Nevada. The complete route was Laarbruch (Germany) – St Mawgan (Cornwall) – Lajes (Azores) – Gander (Newfoundland) – Seymour Johnson (North Carolina) – Bergstrom (Texas) – Nellis (Nevada). The culmination of this navigational spectacular was undertaken on the leg from Bergstrom to Nellis, which was flown (legally!) on a Sunday in a nine-ship formation at 1,500 ft along the length of the Grand Canyon in a diamond nine.

Red Flag has been a huge success for many years, but in the days of the Cold War, it had one disadvantage from a tactical training perspective. Situated in the Nevada desert, it was hardly representative of the conditions that crews could expect to meet in any conflict in the European theatre of operations. By the late 1970s, a similar organization had been established at the Canadian Forces Base at Cold Lake in Alberta, where the exercises were run by the Red Flag directing staff and the Canadian air staff. Buccaneer squadrons were soon asked to join in

Each Victor tanker looked after four Buccaneers for the return to Honington. The five aircraft had tanked to full from a second Victor that returned to Cold Lake. The accompanying Victor filled the Buccaneers for a second time before the formation landed at Goose Bay. The procedure was repeated the following day as they crossed the Atlantic. The formation is seen at 30,000 ft over the forbidding wastes of northern Canada. (*Author*)

the fun, and visits to Cold Lake became an annual event.

The overland Buccaneer squadrons were invited to participate in the third of these so-called 'Maple Flag' exercises, which took place in May 1979. Eight aircraft of 208 Squadron flew the increasingly familiar North Atlantic route, with Victor tankers in support, and staged through Goose Bay to Cold Lake. Crews from XV and 16 Squadrons again formed part of the detachment and flew throughout the exercise. Apart from the Buccaneers, over forty USAF and US Navy aircraft took part, together with twenty-four Canadian aircraft. The format of a Maple Flag exercise was very similar to that of Red Flag, with Aggressor squadrons and simulated ground threats, and there were opportunities to drop weapons although the range area was smaller.

In fact, the Cold Lake Air Weapons Range (the CLAW) was about 100 miles by 40 covered by silver birch and dotted with lakes – a less glamorous venue than the Nellis ranges but nonetheless a realistic opportunity to fly over terrain and targets more akin to those likely to be encountered in Cold War Europe. The range was covered by electronic emitters and anti-aircraft sites (to be avoided), and dummy tanks and airfields (to be attacked). Whilst the targets lacked the elaborate scoring facilities of their Red Flag cousins, the free-flying environment provided excellent value and training opportunities. During a later Maple Flag exercise in May 1981, Squadron Leader Rob Wright of 208 Squadron found himself the leader of a sixty-aircraft 'gorilla' – an attack package for the final sortie of the exercise:

It had been a good fortnight culminating in this last mass launch, by which time tactics and ideas had developed to a very fine pitch. The Buccaneers had been selected to lead this final exercise and, after take-off, we turned north and planned to enter the range at ultra-low level from about 100 miles north with Air National Guard A-7Ds overhead to draw off the fighters while we dashed in from a different direction at 100 ft. The plan worked; we had sneaked in. Ingression now and the pace picks up, accelerating to 540 knots. Trees and lakes a blur at 100 ft and 1 mile every 7 seconds, avoid overflying the lakes (aircraft easy to spot from above) on the approach to the target, an airfield complex. Jinking to avoid missiles locking on, airfield appearing, each of eight crews heading for their own particular aiming points, very aware of the cross-overs as we hit the airfield and all looking to de-conflict and avoid debris. Across the very flat terrain we could see other groups of the attack package – F-111s, F-16s, A-7Ds, F-18s – hitting their associated targets of SAMs, convoys, ammunition dumps, all of the package coordinated across the target area in just a couple of minutes to saturate the defences. Adrenalin pumping, hit the target, accelerate to 580 knots for egress with number two 'hanging-in' for mutual cover. SAM lock-up, jink, break lock, watch for lone pine tree that sticks out above the others in this featureless terrain, see the team appearing from either side as we join the infamous Buccaneer timeline. No talk required here, just confidence in your colleagues in the knowledge that they would appear on time, at the right place, in wide battle-formation for cross-cover.

Back at Cold Lake, mass debrief, videos, good plan, extremely good low-flying and tactics, effective counters, some kills (but not against us), targets hit, very good effort and effective coordination, good results and the Brits seen as being very professional. The old 'Banana jet' had served us well.

Two days later the Squadron returned to UK via Trenton and Goose Bay, where they met up with the Victor tankers ready to provide their usual excellent service. Flying in pairs, each with a tanker in support, the eight Buccaneers arrived back at Honington after a six-hour flight involving two air-to-air refuellings from the Victors.

As the 208 Squadron Buccaneers landed they were welcomed back by a signal from the Air Officer Commanding No. 1 Group, Air Vice-Marshal Mike Knight, informing them that they were to take part in the Tactical Bombing Competition. This did not present a problem until it was discovered it was due to start the following week! After a few sorties to reacclimatise to British weather and some bombing practice on the Wash ranges, four aircraft, supported by squadron ground crew, departed for Lossiemouth to enter the fray with the Jaguars, F-111s and the F-16 'Fighting Falcon' making its debut in Europe. En-route, practice weapons were dropped on the east coast ranges. Running into the target at Cowden, the Flight Commander inadvertently dropped the Boss's suitcase into the sea from the bomb bay of his aircraft – and it didn't even hit the target! Rob Wright was the formation leader on each of the five competition days:

After the 'hiccup' on the way to Lossiemouth, this was a very stimulating exercise, centred on tactical targets at the Spadeadam and Otterburn ranges, with Lightning and Phantom fighter CAPs covering several mandatory 'gates', a point scoring system for 'kills against' and 'kills for' and points for successful bombing on targets at Otterburn. These targets consisted of an airfield and a series of convoys – all protected by radars, missile sites and ground observers. The early sorties involved standard coordinated attacks approaching from each end of the target complex by flying down valleys, but the RAF Regiment Rapier Squadron had set themselves up extremely well on perfect vantage points to cover our approaches into Otterburn. By the time we launched on the final mission, the team had decided we would do something different and put the Rapier teams in their place.

We elected to carry out an unconventional attack from the south, 500 knots in a very tight line-astern formation on a CBU attack, to drop simultaneously on the convoy ranged on the south slopes on the northern side of the range. During the ultra-low transit, our tactics to avoid the fighters revolved around an innate knowledge of what the formation members would do, staying very low, covering each other, widening and, if threatened, splitting and taking separate valleys to rejoin on the timeline just short of the range where we closed up in our 'formation'. We skimmed over the ridge as one unit, spotted the target, bombed on my call (target was deemed completely destroyed) and, immediately off target, each selected a gully that we flew down to escape, weaving, jinking, hiding before joining up on the timeline and heading for Lossie. Hardly a word had been spoken. Most amazing 30 minutes I think I ever had in an aeroplane, and a huge feeling of satisfaction.

In the mass debrief, the comment on the Rapier video had been, 'I can hear them, but I can't . . . see them . . .' followed by an expletive and a single ear-splitting noise – and then silence. And that was it. Not a single kill on the team and four direct hits on the convoy. The same sense of satisfaction and professionalism that we had experienced at the end of Maple Flag. What a month, what flying, what a team and what an aeroplane! The Buccaneer.

Rob Wright fails to mention that he was presented with the award as the top RAF pilot. However, he was the first to acknowledge that it was a crew award and that his navigator, Squadron Leader Roger Stone, shared in the success. On return to Honington at the end of the week-long detachment, the crews were met by their wives, who had produced a large banner heralding the Squadron's success in TBC – the Tactical Baggage Competition as they had christened it!

The Buccaneer continued to prove that it was an outstanding aircraft in both the maritime and overland roles, but the continued use of Second World War vintage bombs and the lack of a precision weapon limited its effectiveness. To fill this major gap in the aircraft's operational effectiveness, the AN/AVQ-23E Pave Spike laser designator was purchased for the RAF in 1979, to give the Service its first laser-guided bomb capability with Paveway LGBs. The recently formed 216 Squadron had been detailed to pioneer the introduction of the system, but its early demise left XV and 208 Squadrons with the task of conducting some of the early trials, codenamed 'Tropical'. The Pave Spike 'pod' was mounted on the port inner pylon and the navigator aimed the laser, using a joystick to keep a cross-wire over the target pictured on the Martel screen. The first trial was flown in October 1979 at Garvie Island, with the aim of testing the compatibility of the system. Both squadrons tossed 1,000-lb HE bombs and provided their own designation. This proved the effectiveness of the system on the Buccaneer and was a very useful introduction for the few crews

The wing-fold mechanism was retained on all RAF aircraft, and provided a great deal of flexibility during parking and hangar storage. The aircraft is fitted with the Westinghouse ALQ 101-10 ECM pod and CBLS. In poor weather, the Lossiemouth lighthouse in the background was a welcome landmark. (*Peter March*)

involved. Although the grounding of the aircraft after the Red Flag accident interrupted the trial, it was resumed in June 1981, and Flight Lieutenant John Plumb was one of the navigators 'selected' to fly the calibration trials. He describes the events of the second Trial 'Tropical':

> The trial was conducted at the West Freugh/Luce Bay range. It involved level drops from 2-3,000 ft as well as toss attacks against a raft target. Target designation was from the ground and the whole attack was closely controlled and measured by telemetry. After a somewhat pedantic brief, we flew our first sortie on 24 June 1981 in XV 352. We carried out the pre-flight checks; the 1,000-lb HES bomb casing was familiar but the kit strapped to the nose and tail were not. On the nose was the guidance and control unit, comprising a laser seeker-head, flight control system and electronics unit and, at the rear a set of pop-out wings and an arming vane. It appeared 'Heath Robinson', with only the 'all-seeing laser eye' resembling hi-tech.
>
> Once airborne, we flew to the range and made contact with the ground controller who, in effect, took over the flying of the aircraft. The pilot had to achieve the parameters precisely and eventually we released our first Paveway II. The result was '50 ft at six and slightly downwind' and the same result with the second bomb. The scientists reviewed the errors and recognised that they had not fully understood the weapon flight-path from toss attacks. At its apogee, the bomb corrected its flight path to centre the received laser energy and therefore it fell below its ideal flight path. Its subsequent progress towards the target was a series of nose-up adjustments to centre the reflected laser energy whilst increasingly losing kinetic energy. The end result, because the 'bang-bang' control system never achieved a perfect solution and the energy level was low, was a short and downwind impact. The answer for the next day's sortie was to direct the laser slightly high and into wind. Sure enough it worked – and the first recommendations of Trial Tropical were written!

Years later, and with an ever increasing emphasis on minimising casualties and collateral damage, the LGB/airborne laser designator

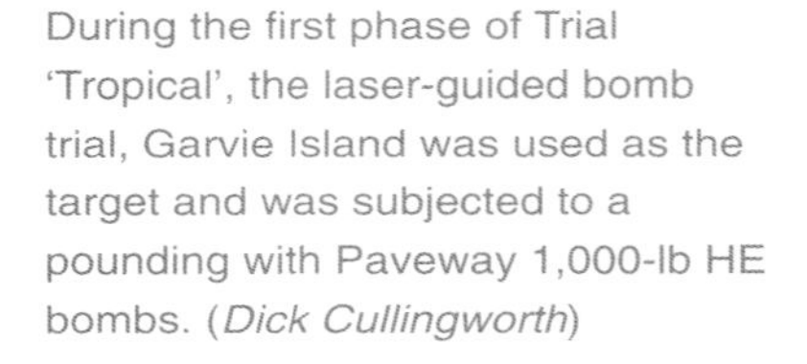

During the first phase of Trial 'Tropical', the laser-guided bomb trial, Garvie Island was used as the target and was subjected to a pounding with Paveway 1,000-lb HE bombs. (*Dick Cullingworth*)

combination had become the weapon system of choice against fixed, point targets by day and night. Even the protagonists would probably not have anticipated the level of success and reliance as a result of those early beginnings in June 1981. Certainly, Terry Heyes and I never appreciated the importance of our work, what it would lead to and the extent to which it would influence bombing philosophy and tactics.

More comprehensive testing followed these early trial sorties and the CTTO-directed Trial Tropical III was carried out in October 1981. This was the final phase of the trial to establish the feasibility of using laser-guided 1,000-lb Paveway bombs in the low-level attack role. Whereas previous phases of the trial had concentrated on releasing the weapons using ground and air designation in an academic range environment, the facilities in the area around the Canadian Air Force base of Cold Lake allowed the practice of operational deliveries using airborne designation. Crews drawn from 16 Squadron flew the majority of Pave Spike designator sorties and 208 Squadron crews flew the Paveway bomber sorties. Squadron Leader 'Dutch' Holland was one of the navigators:

> Our remit was to 'take eighty-four Paveway bombs to Cold Lake, arrange to drop them in a realistic operational delivery mode and prove the viability of the weapon'. We were allocated one month to carry out the task with a team from CTTO to oversee the trial and a team of 'boffins' to set up the telemetry necessary to record the results. Four 208 Squadron crews flew the aircraft to Cold Lake where we were joined by two Germany-based crews to provide the expertise in airborne designation.

Buccaneers pioneered the use of laser designation in the RAF using the Westinghouse AN/AVQ-23 Pave Spike system. The final phase of Trial 'Tropical' was held at the Cold Lake Air Weapons Range in Canada. The two bombers en route to the range are both loaded with four Paveway II 1,000-lb bombs. Accompanying them was the 'spiker' aircraft flown by crews drawn from the RAF Germany squadrons. (*Author*)

All five crews were highly experienced on the Buccaneer and had been involved with the previous weapon trials. We had clearance to fly at 100 ft above ground for both weapons delivery and en route navigation allowing us to practise low-level tactics for delivery from the outset. We all had experience of low-level flying in the north of Canada and were quickly reminded of the hazards of flying over featureless, tree covered terrain – namely the lack of perspective for judgement of height, the occasional dead stump projecting some twenty feet or more from the surrounding trees and, of course, the inevitable problems with accurate navigation over such terrain.

Initially we kept the tactics simple using a pair of aircraft – a designator and a bomber carrying one Paveway bomb. The targets consisted of white sheets of various sizes, erected on poles and set in a clearing and the telemetry equipment was positioned to record the impacts. The idea was to fly towards the target and accelerate to 580 kts at the ten-mile point at which stage the designator aircraft would fall back to one-mile line astern on the leader. Generally the navigator would acquire the target on his scope at about the three-mile point at which time he would call 'contact', allowing the designator aircraft to make a 4 g turn away from the target whilst the cross-hairs were hopefully held firmly over the target and the laser operated. Meanwhile the bomber would establish a three-second pull-up at the appropriate time to toss the bomb into the reflected laser basket, and the weapon would home in to the target under its own inertia.

Anybody vaguely familiar with operational flying and weaponry would immediately realise that the scope for error associated with the above tactic was enormous. Firstly, accurate navigation to the target was paramount, as was early acquisition on the Pave Spike scope. It was soon realised that a great deal of skill was required from the designator navigator not only to identify and acquire the target but, most importantly, to hold the cross-hairs accurately over it during the 4 g escape manoeuvre. The laser head was only ground-stabilised to a limited degree and correction was continually required. The bomber crew had to visually acquire the target to enable a reasonably accurate release of the bomb – otherwise there was a chance that it would not enter the cone of reflected energy.

Towards the end of the trial we were flying realistic sortie profiles at 100 ft throughout, with three aircraft; two bombers and one designator. The two bombers would pull up together tossing their bombs at the target from a range of approximately two miles. The grand finale, and proof of the success of the trial, consisted of launching eight bombs simultaneously against a ten-ft square target – the camera footage was something to behold and the weapon gave us a true stand-off attack capability.

Twenty-one years on, memories of the trial are many. The thrill of ultra-low flying in sometimes marginal weather and the occasional moose getting in the way, the level of skill developed over a relatively short period with a small close-knit team, the punchy ultra-low run in and breaks on the return to Cold Lake and of course a job well done 'paving' the way for future development of laser guided weapons in the RAF. Above all it was a very exciting way of using some of our old war time stock of 1,000-lb freefall bombs, albeit with the addition of sophisticated American technology!

Towards the end of 'Tropical' the bombers were tossing four bombs at the small, 10-ft high white sheet used as a target. One bomb has hit the target and a second is about to score a 'bulls eye.' The top two are close overshoots but would have hit a target just a few feet taller. The trial was a great success and proved the operational effectiveness of the weapon used so successfully ten years later during the Gulf War. (*Dave Herriot*)

Following the outstanding success of Trial Tropical, the RAF Germany squadrons and 208 Squadron adopted the Paveway/Pave Spike LGB attacks as a primary attack option. In a formation of four, two aircraft carried the Pave Spike pod and one Paveway LGB and the other two acted exclusively as 'bombers'. Jaguars were also equipped with the LGB, and 16 Squadron acted as 'spikers' for them in addition to their Buccaneer colleagues. Attacks required very careful coordination between the formation elements, and tactics were practised on the remote weapon range at Garvie Island, where 16 Squadron had opportunities to practise with Buccaneers and Jaguars, and on Red Flag detachments.

By 1983, the UK-based Tornado GR 1 force had started to build up at Honington in order to assume the overland strike role, thus allowing 208 Squadron to retrain for the maritime role and to join 12 Squadron at Lossiemouth on 1 July 1983. At the same time, Tornado GR 1s started to arrive at Laarbruch and XV Squadron amalgamated with 16 Squadron on 1 July 1983 under the command of Wing Commander Eddie Cox. The Germany 'Buccaneer Era' finally came to an end on 29 February 1984, when 16 Squadron was re-equipped with the Tornado. Group Captain Graham Smart MBE, AFC was one of the last Buccaneer Station Commanders of Laarbruch with three previous Buccaneer tours under his belt:

> Much time was spent in RAF Germany improving and improvising in order that the aircraft of 2 ATAF, including the Buccaneer, could operate for as long as possible in a conventional war against the Warsaw Pact. Whatever the validity of our concept in those days, enormous amounts of energy, effort and original thought were put into all aspects of airfield passive and active defence, to enable our aircraft to operate for as long as possible against what was always assumed would be constant and overwhelming air attacks on our airfields. Honed by Minevals, Maxevals and Tacevals, the Squadrons could, and did, continue to operate whilst most of their support assets were progressively stripped from them and they became, by common consent, probably the best organised and most efficient tactical operators in the Central Region.
>
> Nonetheless, an overriding consideration for a real war was the probability of being forced into nuclear operations, and for this the Buccaneer was the only long-range UK strike asset available to COMTWOATAF. There was always the thought that the tasking of the Buccaneers during the conventional phase of operations – many of dubious value in the overall sum of things – and the inevitable losses incurred, might well denude us of the one asset that could prove the vital one in the final resolution of any conflict. The Buccaneer, despite the improvements in fit and weapons, was undoubtedly most at home and most effective over the water. I always felt that against the air defence weapons that would be ranged against us in the Central Region, our best hope of maximising Buccaneer effectiveness was the 'unthinkable' and, whilst hoping that it would never happen, doing one's best to prepare for it. That the Laarbruch Buccaneer Wing kept a credible capability in both conventional and nuclear operations over many years speaks volumes for all the men and women who served there in every capacity – and also of course is to the eternal credit of the ever flexible, capable and much loved Buccaneer.

The final phase of RAF Germany Buccaneer operations was to amalgamate XV and 16 Squadrons. The aircraft carried the badges of both squadrons with the 16 Squadron 'saint' superimposed over the familiar Roman numeral badge of XV Squadron. The combined squadron was withdrawn on 29 February 1984 when the aircraft were re-allocated amongst the UK-based units. (*Ian Black*)

With the demise of the RAF Germany Buccaneer squadrons, and their laser designation capability for LGB-armed aircraft in 2 ATAF, the only readily available option was to give the Buccaneer OCU a war role to provide the necessary laser designation. So, Buccaneers of 237 OCU were given a war role of providing a Pave Spike 'marker' force for RAF Germany Jaguar and, later, Tornado squadrons. The OCU was assigned to support Option 'Lima', a 2 ATAF plan to attack high-value targets such as bridges and other lines of communication. Four aircraft were assigned to this role, and they regularly deployed to Laarbruch to practise tactics on numerous alert exercises. The aircraft fit was a Pave Spike pod on the port inner pylon, a Sidewinder AIM-9G on the port outer, a wing tank on the starboard inner and an ALQ 101-10 ECM pod on the outer. Four retard bombs were carried in the bomb bay, to be used as that old 'last ditch' option should a fighter appear from behind, and chaff was installed in the airbrake.

Two Buccaneers joined up with four bombers and the 'package' transited at low level to the target area, with one Buccaneer 'spiking' for two Jaguars or Tornadoes. The attack aircraft set up a profile to toss the LGBs from low level towards the target. Each Buccaneer crew carried out an individual run to the target, with the pilot responsible for identifying the target. Once the navigator had been 'conned' onto the target, he marked it and, at an appropriate time, switched on the laser. Flight Lieutenant Norman Browne was heavily involved in the development of Pave Spike tactics, and he describes the technique:

> The success of an attack from low level was all dependent on the correct positioning of the 'spiker' who had to be behind the bombers but able to see them and the target. We have to remember that we had no software in the early days and all tactics were done on manual timing. Having marked the

237 OCU was given the war role of providing Pave Spike 'marker' for RAF Jaguars and 322 Squadron of the Royal Netherlands Air Force. Regular visits were made to the Dutch airfields, and this aircraft taxis to a dispersal at Twenthe. The ALQ 101-10 pod and Sidewinder can be seen. The Pave Spike pod was carried on the port inner pylon. (*Jelle Sjoerdsma*)

A Pave-Spike-equipped Buccaneer of 237 OCU accompanies two Sea Harriers of 899 Squadron to provide laser designation for a live Paveway drop at Garvie Island. (*Tom Eeles*)

target, we had to work out when to switch on the laser so that the bomb was in the bracket. Designation too early resulted in the LGB falling well short, and designation too late gave insufficient time for the primitive 'bang bang' control system on the bomb to guide it correctly with the result that an overshoot occurred. Once the navigator had the target marked and was holding it, the pilot could manoeuvre up to 4 g and he had freedom to evade and escape. Once the laser was designating, it was another twenty to twenty-five seconds before the bomb impacted, which could seem a very long time in certain circumstances.

A very strong supporter of the Option 'Lima' concept was Group Captain Nigel Walpole, a senior air staff officer at HQTWOATAF and a former Buccaneer pilot. He was aware that the RNethAF had acquired a stock of LGBs but had no designation capability. With his assistance, a NATO squadron exchange was organised between 237 OCU and the Dutch 322 Squadron, whose home was at Leeuwarden, and trials were conducted at Garvie Island. As a consequence of this very successful exercise, 237 OCU was formally assigned to support 322 Squadron on Option 'Lima'. In 1988 they were also tasked to provide support to 315 Squadron at Twenthe and regular joint exercises were flown. The OCU continued in the specialist role until its disbandment in October 1991.

CHAPTER 8

Lossiemouth Maritime Wing

Prior to the arrival at Honington of the Tornado GR1 units, a decision had been taken to move the UK-based Buccaneer force to its spiritual home at Lossiemouth, which had itself been transferred to the RAF in September 1972. First to move was 12 Squadron in November 1980, and 208 arrived on 1 July 1983, when it transferred to No. 18 (Maritime) Group and was assigned to SACLANT. Finally, 237 OCU moved north in October 1984. As the Navy had discovered, Lossiemouth was an ideal location for the maritime squadrons, being close to its likely wartime operational area and to the excellent local air-to-ground weapons range at Tain. Although small – some forty aircraft – the Wing provided SACLANT with his only dedicated maritime strike/attack squadron, and it became the major anti-shipping force in the North-East Atlantic region.

Throughout the early 1980s the 'blue water' Soviet Navy continued to develop as a potent force, and the arrival of increasingly effective SA-N systems posed a very serious threat to any attacking aircraft that approached inside 15 miles. The tactics of the Buccaneer Wing had changed little from the Honington days and were based on third-party shadow support supplemented by Buccaneer probes and followed by a coordinated attack. Both squadrons were equipped with the AR Martel for defence suppression, with 12 Squadron firing TV Martels and 208 Squadron tossing LGBs for precision attacks. The availability of the LGBs significantly increased accuracy but the bombers remained very vulnerable. It came as a relief to the aircrews of both squadrons when, in 1983, plans were announced to update a batch of aircraft with a modern navigation system, improved radios and new ECM equipment. Of even greater significance was the announcement that the aircraft would be made compatible with the new British Aerospace Sea Eagle anti-shipping missile. However, the new capability would not become available for another two or three years. In the meantime, tactics employing the old weapons had continually to be refined, but continued to be based on the 'Alpha' attacks devised some twelve years earlier.

For 12 Squadron, little had changed over the years. The Squadron continued to employ both versions of Martel, and formations continued to use target information from Nimrods and to adopt modified versions of the 'Alpha' attacks, with AR Martels fired for defence suppression followed by a salvo of TV Martels. The arrival of 208 Squadron, equipped with AR Martel and the Paveway LGBs, involved some changes to the standard 'Alpha' attacks used for tossing 1,000-lb bombs. Two aircraft carried AR Martel and they

Opposite: By July 1983, 208 Squadron had left Honington to join 12 Squadron and form the Lossiemouth Maritime Wing. (*Mike Scarffe*)

359

were fired if the target continued to transmit with its radars. The bombers, armed with two Paveway 1,000-lb LGBs, tossed the bombs from 2–3 miles with the 'spiker' in long trail. Once the target was marked, the 'spiker' turned away at some 8 miles and the gimballed head of the Pave Spike continued to track the target as the laser was fired until the bombs impacted. The bombers were particularly vulnerable throughout the profile unless the AR Martels had been successful, and during the recovery they would have dropped chaff and made the appropriate selections on the ALQ 101-10 ECM pod. However, against less well-defended targets, such as intelligence-gathering ships, vital re-supply support ships and amphibious shipping, the LGB provided a heavy weight of bombs with accuracy not previously attainable.

Aircrew flying on maritime squadrons during peacetime and periods of transition-to-war enjoyed a big advantage over their overland colleagues. There were regular opportunities to come face-to-face with the threat and to carry out photographic and radar reconnaissance. Buccaneer aircrew had been able to view the formidable array of Soviet warships from the 1960s and had never failed to be impressed by the huge advances in their capability. It could be a

Flying from Lossiemouth put the Buccaneers much closer to their potential area of operations, but the support of the tanker force remained crucial. The advent of new weapons and self-defence aids occupied the Buccaneer's wing stations, and wing tanks were used less frequently. As with the Victor tanker, the VC 10 carried an air-to-air refuelling pod on both wings. (*Malcolm English*)

Regular contact was made with ships of the Soviet Navy, but it was very unusual for Buccaneers to intercept their aircraft. Two aircraft of 12 Squadron intercepted this Bear of the Soviet Naval Air Force during exercises in 1987. (*Keith Moore*)

chilling experience to approach a *Sverdlov* cruiser, the Buccaneer's intended adversary in the earlier days, although the later generation of cruisers and destroyers encountered on almost every exercise posed a far greater threat. Such encounters occurred throughout the North Atlantic and in the Mediterranean, and a great deal of intelligence was gathered, in addition to reminding the crews of the scale and capability of the threat. The late Squadron Leader Chas Wrighton of 12 Squadron wrote:

> After a practice attack against a friendly ship we approached another target and slipped into trail as we identified a *Kresta 2*. As we flew round the ship we made a note of the time and her position. Viewed up close, she presented a formidable sight, bristling with armament catering for all aspects of naval warfare. Twin multi-barrel rocket launchers, torpedo tubes and the large quadruple anti-submarine SS-N-14 missiles mounted either side of the bridge in inclined boxes. More pertinent to our eyes were the four anti-aircraft guns and the SA-N-3 surface-to-air missile launchers that could be aimed in our direction. The top of the ship was covered with radars and our ears told us that electronic eyes as well as human eyes were pointing towards us, assessing us as we assessed them. We carefully scanned the ship, looking for any modifications that might have been incorporated, and searching for any non-standard fitments or new equipments. Nothing out of the ordinary – and sea and air power eyed each other respectfully before we departed.

During late 1983, the situation in Lebanon became critical, and air support for the British contingent of the United Nations peace-keeping force was considered necessary. Buccaneers equipped with Pave Spike and Paveway LGBs were deemed to be the most suitable for precision attacks against terrorist targets in built-up areas, and six aircraft were tasked to deploy to RAF Akrotiri in Cyprus and be prepared to participate in Operation 'Pulsator'. The aircraft were modified to carry ALE-40 chaff/flare dispensers and AIM 9-G or AIM 9-L Sidewinder air-to-air missiles. Once the aircraft were established in Cyprus plans were drawn up for a series of sorties to demonstrate the RAF's capability with Phantoms and Lightnings based at Akrotiri to provide fighter cover. The Buccaneer Detachment Commander was Wing Commander Ben Laite, OC 208 Squadron, and he relates the events:

> A Forward Air Controller (FAC) and Tactical Air Control Party were flown out to Beirut to join the troops of the 14/21 Hussars, accommodated in a block of flats and a rudimentary tactical plan was devised. The aim was to ensure that the Buccaneers could react in a timely fashion to any warning of a threat from hostile ground forces to the British contingent in the flats in Beirut. Thus the crews and aircraft were established on a five-minute standby roster at Akrotiri. On a call for action from the Beirut HQ, the crews would launch, and fly to a predetermined entry point to cross the Lebanese coast. By then, it was expected that more precise target information would be available and the Buccaneers would toss their LGBs under the instruction of an FAC equipped with a laser-target marker. Effective communications were vital.
>
> After some cautious testing and an initial ground reconnaissance in Beirut, it was decided to launch four trial sorties. Two pairs of aircraft were launched on 11 and 13 September and the aircraft transited through the US Fleet Protection Zone, which needed much coordination, so we put a navigator on board the carrier to act as a liaison officer. On coasting in, the aircraft flew across the British block of flats, turned north, flew to the harbour in the north of the city then reversed for another over-fly and departed back through the US Fleet. The brief was to stay as low as possible and keep the Pave Spike video-recorders active throughout the overland stages. The crews flew their missions exactly according to the briefing – hence the rapidly coined phrase, 'Real men fly through Beirut, not over it!'
>
> Post-sortie debriefing gleaned as much intelligence and useful information as possible from the crews. One significant report ascertained that small arms gunfire was heard as the aircraft transited the city. The sorties were deemed to have been highly successful. Not only were the British troops mightily cheered to see British aircraft in such a spirited display of support, but also the aircrews themselves had gained valuable experience in practising the sortie profile, a feature, which would be very valuable in any genuine emergency. Furthermore, the various factions in Beirut were now quite forcefully aware that British air support had arrived.

The Buccaneer detachment maintained a constant state of readiness with armed aircraft, from dawn

Two Buccaneers of 12 Squadron deployed to the Falkland Islands in May 1983 to test a rapid reinforcement plan. They staged through Ascension Island and used air-to-air refuelling support, arriving after sixteen hours' flying time. One is seen here parked in a readiness hangar at RAF Mount Pleasant. (*Ian Macfadyen*)

Pairs of Buccaneers made over-flights of Beirut on 11 September 1983 as a show of force and morale booster for the British troops. Newspaper headlines announced that 'RAF jets fly flag at 50 ft over Beirut.' Six overflights were made, with the last on 13 September. (*via Peter March*)

Operation 'Pulsator' was mounted to support British troops in Lebanon and six Buccaneers deployed to RAF Akrotiri. A constant state of readiness was maintained with aircraft armed with Pave Spike and Paveway 1,000-lb LGBs and an impressive array of defensive aids, including the ALQ 101–10 ECM pod, an AIM 9-L Sidewinder and ALE-40 chaff and flare dispensers. (*Author's collection*)

till dusk, until March 1984. The detachment maintained proficiency by flying sorties over southern Cyprus, and some maritime sorties over the Mediterranean and weapons profiles were practised on the Episkopi Air Weapons Range. Crews were rotated from Lossiemouth, and some Pave Spike specialists from the RAF Germany Buccaneer squadrons joined the detachment. It was withdrawn on 26 March 1984, when the Buccaneers were flown home to Lossiemouth via Sigonella and Nice. The operation had been a success although no further sorties had been flown in anger.

By 1986 there were significant developments in the Buccaneer force, with each squadron occupying the recently completed third-generation HAS sites at Lossiemouth, and the first aircraft left for the British Aerospace plant at Woodford for the embodiment of the avionics update programme required to fulfil Air Staff Requirement 1012. The package included a new Plessey ASR 889 radio and an upgraded RWR (the digital Sky Guardian 200), which included E–J band receivers housed in the wing-mounted pods previously used for the wide-band homer. The original fore and aft antennae on top of the fin were retained for the C–D band detection aerials. AN/ALE-40 chaff and flare dispensers were fitted, with the chaff dispensers 'scabbed' on to the outside of the outer wing pylons and the flares under the jet-pipes. Full compatibility for the Sidewinder AIM 9-G or 9L was also included. However, the central element was the fitting of an inertial navigation platform for use in conjunction with the Sea Eagle. Squadron Leader Mike Scarffe explains the need for an inertial navigation (IN) system:

> The IN system chosen was the Ferranti FIN 1063. It provided the Sea Eagle with essential navigation inputs, such as target range and bearing at launch to make it a 'fire and forget' missile. With third-party targeting, normally a Nimrod MPA, it was possible to programme the missile to pop up 10 miles from the target when its active radar seeker searched for and detected the target before descending to a few feet above the sea and slammed into the target less than two minutes after first alerting the ship. All this depended on an accurate target position from the shadowing aircraft and an accurate IN platform to store the information. That was the requirement for

Part of the ASR 1012 update for the aircraft was the digital Sky Guardian 200 radar warning receiver housed in the two bullets at the top of the fin. The E–J band receivers were housed in the two former wide-band homer aerials on the outer wing. The photograph of the 12 Squadron Gulf War veteran XX 885 provides a particularly good view of the laser seeker head and the large 'bang-bang' tail unit strapped to a 1,000-lb bomb. (*Peter March*)

Introduction of the Sea Eagle anti-ship missile gave the Buccaneer Wing a quantum jump in capability. Both squadrons were equipped with the sea-skimming missile in 1986–7. (*MOD/Crown copyright*)

Allied to the upgraded navigation suite, the Buccaneer had a true 'fire and forget' capability and a formation of aircraft launching four missiles each could swamp a ship's defences without the aircraft having to penetrate the target's weapons engagement zone. The missile was equipped with a radio altimeter allowing it to fly at 10 ft. (*BAe Systems*)

> the IN and the subsequent luxury for Buccaneer navigators, knowing exactly where they were to a few yards, was a pure bonus. Of course, this bonus was put to good use and enabled formations to fly huge splits over the sea with amazing accuracy and then to rejoin the formation at any pre-briefed point and time. This gave enormous flexibility for inventing new tactics and delivering weapons on different axes.

Sea Eagle was a long-range, anti-shipping missile powered by a turbo-jet engine. With a range of 60 miles, four times that of Martel, Sea Eagle was a genuine 'fire-and-forget' missile which followed a sea-skimming flight profile, remaining radar silent until it estimated that it had penetrated the radar horizon of the target, at which point it began to climb. It then switched on its I-band active homing head, selected its target and resumed its sea-skimming profile before hitting the target 10 ft above the water line. As a true 'sea skimmer', flying at 10 ft, it was a very difficult target to engage. The 506-lb blast fragmentation warhead was significantly more powerful than that of Martel. Each aircraft could carry four missiles, which, when launched simultaneously, gave a formation tremendous firepower greatly in excess of any Martel-equipped formation. No. 208 Squadron was operational with Sea Eagle at the end of 1986, and twelve months later, the first fully updated aircraft (XV 161) arrived on 12 Squadron, which became fully operational with the new missile during 1988. Squadron Leader Tony Lunnon-Wood echoed the views of all his Buccaneer colleagues:

> There was a standing joke in the maritime Buccaneer force that if you didn't get airborne on the first wave against a Soviet SAG you would spend the rest of the war grounded due to lack of aeroplanes. The probability of returning from an iron bomb or Martel attack against a modern ship was slim – more importantly we would probably be engaged well before releasing our antiquated ordnance.
>
> The Buccaneer force had been awaiting the introduction of Sea Eagle with impatience. For too long we had been attacking ships with iron bombs and a very temperamental Anglo-French missile. Both weapons were outdated but, more importantly, relied on the attacking aircraft breaking the radar horizon to launch or release. Our planned attrition rate against Soviet SAGs was eye watering and, come the war, a Buccaneer maritime crew's longevity was zero.
>
> With the advent of the Sea Eagle missile and associated avionics update, we had the capability to carry out coordinated attacks against surface ships from multiple axes, and to ensure missile strike times within 10 seconds despite formation splits of up to 40 miles. The QWIs had the chance to design tactics that would work in any weather day or night, to inflict maximum damage with minimum risk to the Buccaneer formation – a task that was immensely satisfying, knowing we had become a silent, potent threat to any SAG. Tactics concentrated on saturating ship defences with the maximum number of missiles in the shortest possible time from a twin-axis attack. A programme in the IN allowed the navigators to set waypoints to ensure a formation split to attack with twenty-four missiles arriving within a 10-second block!
>
> During exercises, after 'firing', the aircraft would then fly the missile profile to a point overhead the ship to confirm timing accuracy. It was a shocking revelation to our Navy friends and aptly demonstrated during maritime exercises. With Nimrod support, six Buccaneers could arrive overhead a ship within 10 seconds on two different axes. The ships weapons officer gleefully informed us, by radio, that we had been in radar contact at 21 miles and the picket ship had engaged a target before re-engaging with her close-in systems. When asked how many simulated missile launches were fired by the target, the answer came back as six. An ecstatic Buccaneer pilot replied to a stunned sailor with a cry of 'Navy 6, RAF 24!' When it was subsequently explained that each radar blip was in fact four sea-skimming missiles it suddenly became very apparent that the attack capability of the Buccaneer force had taken a massive leap forward, and that the survivability of a ship against air attack could no longer be taken for granted.
>
> We continued to fly missile profiles, not only for our satisfaction but also to convince the target ships that we were in the area because, with 'over-the-horizon-targeting', we could launch twenty-four missiles way beyond the radar horizon and return to base without the ship having any sort of contact with a six-ship Buccaneer package. The age of the silent ship killer had well and truly arrived. We had the ability to project our personality over vast distances in total silence with devastating accuracy.

Perhaps the peak capability of Sea Eagle tactics was that offered by the night attack. Squadron

Wing Commander Tom Eeles, Squadron Commander of 237 OCU, receives his 2,000 Buccaneer hour badge from his deputy, Squadron Leader Jim Barker. A close examination of the left sleeve of his flying suit suggests that the Wing Commander has pre-empted the event! (*Tom Eeles*)

For over twenty years the Nimrod provided targeting information to Buccaneer formations. Over the years the techniques were developed and a very close understanding developed between the two forces. They rarely met over the oceans, but two Buccaneers pose with their colleagues of the 'kipper fleet'. (*Rick Phillips*)

Leader Rick Phillips, who was the pilot Flight Commander on 208 Squadron at the time, was tasked with putting together, training and leading a constituted six-aircraft formation to carry out Sea Eagle attacks against deep-water targets at night. He explains:

> Initially, I had a great deal of trouble finding willing volunteers for this task – not surprising really when you consider that each sortie was to include over two hours in close formation in the dark at 300 ft, with night tanking thrown in to spice things up! Mike Scarffe was my trusted navigator for this period and we devised the tactics and worked up a sound team, with Tony Lunnon-Wood and his nav, Pete Binham, as our deputy lead. Some of the work-up sortie debriefs were almost as tiring as the flights themselves, but it all came together in September 1988 during Exercise 'Teamwork' when we finally experienced the satisfaction of success. The culmination of our efforts was a copybook six-ship attack. We were totally undetected, until a visual sighting by the target ship, as we flew the missile profile after simulated release of the twenty-four missiles, the whole sortie having been ZIPLIP [radio silent] until that point, including the air-to-air refuelling with a pair of Victor tankers. I doubt this was ever repeated, but it felt good to have done it.

The need for third-party targeting was always a key element of successful attacks against shipping, and the methods devised with radar-reconnaissance Victors during the early exercises in 1970 appeared archaic but they had laid the foundations for all the later, upgraded techniques. The enhanced capabilities of the Nimrod had considerably improved the techniques and accuracies, but the combination of the Nimrod and the new Buccaneer with its avionics upgrade brought the 'shadowing' business to new levels of effectiveness. Excellent joint work between 12 Squadron and RAF Kinloss-based 120 Squadron in building up the surface picture and tactical direction for the Buccaneers, resulted in the joint award of the prestigious Wilkinson Sword.

One of the new young pilots joining the Buccaneer force in the summer of 1989 was Flying Officer Niall Watson, and his arrival heralded a unique occasion that would never be repeated. He explains:

> I remember my flying course 'posting party' at the Tactical Weapons Unit very clearly, in particular the surprise at the announcement that I was posted to the Buccaneer. It quickly dawned on me that I would be following in my father's footsteps – flying the same aircraft that he had flown some twenty years earlier, and memories of sitting in a Buccaneer cockpit aged seven during a XV Squadron families day came flooding back. Over the years he had told me a lot about the mighty aircraft and how it was a joy to fly and, now, I was going to get the chance to find out and was very excited by the prospect. I phoned Dad straight away with my news and, of course, he was delighted and very proud to have his youngest son flying the Bucc. He sent me a black and white photo of the instrument panel and, when I reached the OCU, I remember thinking that it hadn't changed much! When I flew the aircraft for the first time, I began to understand why he had held it in such high esteem. As he'd said, at low level and high speed, it was solid as a rock and a superb bombing platform. In the circuit at low speed, well that was another story . . .
>
> I flew with 12 Squadron for four years before being posted to the Tornado, but I returned with Dad to Lossiemouth for the 'Final Fling' where it was finally brought home to me how he was regarded by his former colleagues. I was amazed at the number of people who came up to him saying that their tour with him had been the highlight of their time on the Bucc. Thinking back, my only regret is that I didn't take the opportunity to get him airborne once again for a constituted crew of 'father and son'. That would have been a first, and last, in the history of the Buccaneer force.

By late 1990, the two Buccaneer squadrons had been working together as a Maritime Wing for over seven years, and the avionics update and the introduction of Sea Eagle had made it a very potent anti-shipping strike force. However, world events then took a dramatic turn and the Buccaneer found itself at the centre of the world stage in a most unlikely role for an ultra-low-level, high-speed ship-killer. Iraqi forces invaded Kuwait in August 1990.

To celebrate the thirtieth anniversary of the first flight of the aircraft, thirty Buccaneers of the Lossiemouth Wing went on parade on 30 April 1988. They are parked on the disused runway with the Station Gate Guardian, an ex-Royal Navy Mark 1 on the end. (*Dave Bolsover*)

The green lightning flash on the mid-grey base were the special markings chosen by 12 Squadron to commemorate the Squadron's seventy-fifth anniversary on 14 February 1990. The aircraft used was XX 894. (*Ian Black*)

For the deployment to the Gulf, aircraft were hastily painted in 'desert pink', using a 'removable temporary finish' providing a very effective camouflage. The state of XW 530 a few weeks after returning to Lossiemouth indicates that the description was appropriate. (*Ian Black*)

CHAPTER 9

The Gulf War

Following Saddam Hussein's invasion of Kuwait, the Royal Air Force rapidly built up a powerful air force in the region as part of the Allied Coalition; but there was no role, at first, for the Buccaneer, despite its being the only laser marking aircraft in service with the RAF. However, the recently appointed Station Commander of Lossiemouth, Group Captain Jon Ford, and his Squadron Commanders decided that it would be prudent to review the capabilities and investigate high-level 'spiking', in addition to continuing with low-level tactics. The AOC of No. 18 Group, Air Marshal Sir Michael Stear, agreed and the two squadrons carried out the necessary work and were soon able to report that the technique worked well. Shortly afterwards, hostilities started and Tornadoes commenced low-level airfield attacks, during which several aircraft were lost. Once it was apparent that the Iraqi Air Force was effectively grounded, the Tornadoes commenced bombing from medium level with Second World War vintage, unguided 1,000-lb bombs. Meanwhile, the Royal Navy was working up ships to deploy to the Gulf, and 12 Squadron was deployed to Gibraltar and 208 to St Mawgan to assist in this programme. On 22 January 1991, the AOC and Jon Ford flew to St Mawgan to visit 208 Squadron, where Sir Michael confirmed that there was still no requirement for the Buccaneers, although he favoured their use. Jon Ford returned to Lossiemouth later that day and landed late at night, to be told that he was needed urgently at the Operations Centre. He takes up the story:

> I took a secure phone call from HQ Strike Command and they asked one question 'How quickly could we get a squadron to the Gulf?' Life is full of surprises! I explained that much would depend on how quickly we could recover the aircraft and personnel from Gibraltar and St Mawgan, bearing in mind, at this stage, that all the air transport was tied up supporting the actual war. I was told there would be no problem with transport, to which I said I thought we would be ready in three days from when they got back to

Tristar tankers supported the Buccaneers that deployed to the Gulf in pairs on a nine-hour non-stop flight. (*Rick Phillips*)

base. Looking back, this was a bit of a wild guess, as I had no real idea as to what modifications would be needed on the aircraft.

The next three days were frenetic with the two squadrons returning immediately from their detachments and we set about modifying twelve aircraft. They needed IFF Mode 4, Have Quick II secure radios, new chaff and flare dispensers and a complete re-spray into 'Gulf pink'. One of the first decisions was, should it be a squadron or a wing deployment? With only three days to go, I felt it was vital that we had the strongest possible team and we should choose the crews from across the Wing; and the AOC supported this approach. After the war there was great discussion within the RAF about the merits of each approach. Many armchair experts claimed it should always be a squadron but they did not have to send a team to war at three day's notice to do a task which we had practised of our own volition, but which was not part of our normal training schedule – and at a time when we had just lost seven Tornadoes. I am convinced that, in the circumstances, my decision was correct. The proof of the pudding is that we sent twelve aircraft and twenty crews, had a most successful war and recovered twelve aircraft and twenty crews.

> The question arose as to who should command the detachment and I felt that this should be OC 208 Squadron, Wing Commander Bill Cope, who had the experience of the Pave Spike role and was a very experienced Buccaneer pilot. The aircrew were drawn from the two squadrons and the OCU, and the twenty selected crews had a busy couple of days, not least being injected against copious ills. The first three aircraft left at 4.00 a.m. on Saturday 26 January on their nine-hour flight to Muharraq in Bahrain. Some crews plus 230 ground crew had already left by Hercules. We had made our three days, including the recovery from Gibraltar and St Mawgan, which was a tremendous achievement by the entire Station personnel.

So, after thirty years of continuous service, one of the most outstanding low-level bombers was finally going to war, at high level! When asked why such an old aircraft was being sent to the Gulf, the Secretary of State for Defence was quoted as saying, 'Because we need to improve the standard of precision bombing.' Some accolade. A response more in keeping with the somewhat irreverent tradition of the Buccaneer force came from Bill Cope himself. On landing at Muharraq he was immediately surrounded by radio and TV reporters anxious to ask exactly that question. His reply was a classic: 'My old grandmother is getting on a bit,' he was reported as saying, 'but you wouldn't want to mess with her!'

The aircraft left Lossiemouth in pairs over three days flying a nine-hour direct flight with Tristar tanker support. The first six aircraft arrived in Muharraq by 28 January and immediately commenced a week-long intensive training programme. With air supremacy firmly established, the priority for the Tornadoes had changed to interdicting the supply lines of the Iraqi Army, and bridges spanning the Rivers Euphrates and Tigris became priority targets. On 2 February, seven days after arriving in theatre and just ten since the decision to deploy, the first mission was flown, with two Buccaneers 'spiking' for four Tornadoes bombing the Al Suwaira road bridge. Leading the first Buccaneer war sortie was Bill Cope and his navigator Flight Lieutenant Carl Wilson, with Flight Lieutenant Glen Mason and Squadron Leader Norman Browne in the second aircraft. Norman Browne was a highly experienced Buccaneer navigator who had been involved in the development of Pavespike since its introduction into RAF service twelve years earlier, and he was appointed the detachment's 'spike leader'. He explains the first mission:

> Two of us took off with four Tornadoes of XV Squadron and we headed to the Victor or VC 10 tankers operating over Saudi Arabia south of the Iraqi border. After tanking, we made for the border, with a fighter escort, and checked in with AWACS by which time we had already been airborne for over two hours. In effect, we operated as two sections with one Buccaneer to a pair of Tornadoes and this had the advantage of providing redundancy if one of the 'spikers' became unserviceable. We flew above 20,000 ft and sat five miles behind our pair of Tornadoes closing up as we neared the target. The IN was good, but the pilot had to map read to positively identify the target, at which point he lowered the nose gently and put the sight on the bridge. My Pave Spike was slaved to his sight and once I had the target I called 'happy' and he was free to manoeuvre and keep an eye on the Tornadoes. Once they had released their bombs, they climbed away to head back to the tanker, while I marked the target and fired the laser after 5 or 6 seconds. The time of flight of the bombs was about 30 seconds, which seemed an age. All the time I had to be listening to the RWR and ready to use the ECM suite, since all the switches were in the back. With the video screen, I could immediately evaluate the results of the attack, with the experts back at base carrying out a detailed bomb-damage assessment after we landed. After the attack we immediately left the area to return to base. Unlike the Tornadoes, we didn't need to tank on the way home – so it was direct to Muharraq, avoiding the missile engagement zones and monitoring all the warning gear.

This sortie set the pattern for many others, and the arrival of six more Buccaneers by 8 February

As soon as the Buccaneers arrived in the Gulf region a period of intensive training with the Tornado GR 1s was started. The first operation was flown a few days later on 2 February 1991, just seven days after arriving in theatre. Bombing attacks with Paveway LGBs were flown at medium level, with one Pave Spike Buccaneer accompanying two Tornado GR 1s. Towards the end of the war, the Buccaneers carried a Paveway bomb and carried out self-designated attacks once the Tornadoes had bombed and returned to base. (*Norman Browne*)

A feature of the Gulf War was the re-appearance of nose artwork, and many believe that the Buccaneers displayed the most imaginative. All aircraft were named after local malt whiskies and all but one displayed a 'Sky Pirates' skull and cross bones on the port side. Seven aircraft displayed more typical nose art on the starboard side, all the creation of Corporal Ken Letham. Bomb symbols indicated the number of successful 'spiking' operations. (*Rick Phillips*)

allowed more targets to be attacked. Lessons were learned quickly as the techniques used had never been practised before. Initially, the navigators were told to aim at the abutments of the bridge targets, despite the squadron experts claiming that it would be more effective to aim at the bridge supports. Within a few days, higher authority reversed their orders and navigators were told to aim at the supports! It was also the first time that most of the aircrew had flown in such large 'packages' with fighters, AWACS, Wild Weasels, ECM aircraft and tanker forces all flying in support of the attack formations. Needless to say, none had previously experienced listening to enemy radars triggering the RWR or seeing surface-to-air missiles launched. The Pave Spike was a day-only system and cloud occasionally interfered with an attack, but twenty-four bridges were attacked with great success. As it became increasingly apparent that the Iraqi Air Force would not take to the air, the Sidewinders were

Many targets were in the centre of heavily built-up areas and only precision weapons could be considered. The main road bridge in Al Nasiriyah has been destroyed and a secondary bridge has just been struck. The availability of the Pave Spike video provided instant battle-damage assessment. (*Norman Browne*)

removed from the Buccaneers and each carried a Paveway 1,000-lb LGB. After the Tornado attack was complete, the Buccaneers had sufficient fuel to linger in the target area and drop self-designated bombs from a 40° dive attack before departing directly back to base. A real multi-role capability! To ensure a higher probability of success, tactics were devised to drop bombs from a 60° dive. Rick Phillips explains:

> One particularly satisfying sortie for my navigator, Harry Hyslop, and me was the demolition of a primary target, which had been missed by one of our Tornadoes. We were tasked to re-attack the target and the night before, being very conscious of the criticality of the narrow 45° laser basket, Harry and I invited our Staff QWI advisor, Terry Yarrow, to our hotel room for a wee dram. We then asked him to do some 'back of a fag packet' calculations, to see if we could go for a steeper dive angle, nearer 60°, in order to guarantee getting our own bombs in the laser basket. This, of course, was outside the Release to Service limits for bomb release, but we were not going to get that changed overnight. Terry assured us that the bomb would release with no problems, so we carried out our own 'trial' over the target the next day. It was a resounding success, a tactic we subsequently went on to repeat. One undesirable aspect of the steep dive was seeing the flak from below, as well as from above. After that, I realised that dropping a 28-lb practice bomb at Tain would never be quite the same again!

As the success of the interdiction war grew and the number of bridges decreased, the LGB attacks transferred, on 12 February, to destroying Iraqi Air Force installations. The Tornadoes and Buccaneers were tasked to destroy hardened aircraft shelters, petroleum sites, weapon storage dumps and hangars. Later in the month, the Tornadoes started to receive the thermal imaging airborne laser designators (TIALD) for self-

The Gulf War Buccaneer Detachment pose in front of two Buccaneers armed ready for another operational sortie. Wing Commander Bill Cope, Officer Commanding 208 Squadron and Detachment Commander, stands in front of his team. (*Bill Cope*)

The ground crew performed wonders under difficult conditions, and no sorties were lost due to the unavailability of aircraft. The nose has been folded back to give access to the weapons release computer as the nose undercarriage is inspected before the next flight. (*Rick Phillips*)

designation, and this released the Buccaneers to add their own considerable weight of bombs to the counter-air campaign. As the day for the beginning of the ground war approached, there was a fear that the Iraqi Air Force might make one last attempt to influence the war. As a result, their southern airfields were targeted and the Buccaneers made a major contribution. Perhaps the most newsworthy of these was an opportunity attack on 27 February, the last day of operations, at Shayka Mazhar airfield. After supporting a Tornado attack, transport aircraft were seen on the ground and the Buccaneers attacked them in a steep dive, each dropping two Paveway 1,000-lb bombs. One pair hit a Cub transport. Although the bombs failed to explode, 2,000 lb of iron at terminal velocity is very effective! The second, marked by the Squadron Commander's navigator, Carl Wilson, hit a captured Kuwaiti Hercules and destroyed it. A fitting climax to the final sortie.

Throughout the detachment, the ground crew worked wonders. Under the outstanding leadership of Squadron Leaders George Baber and David Tasker they achieved an unbelievable record of 100 per cent serviceability under very difficult conditions. By the end of the war, over 200 sorties had been flown and there was always a spare aircraft in case of unserviceability. The Buccaneers dropped forty-eight LGBs and 'spiked' 169 for the Tornadoes. As all aircrew know well, the ground crews have always played a vital supportive role, one that becomes even more important in wartime. They are a familiar face to strap the crew in, offer a word of support and comfort and wave them away, and they are the first to welcome them back and share in the success. Without them, there would have been very little success.

On 17 March 1991, the twelve Buccaneers flew back non-stop to Lossiemouth, air-to-air refuelling three times during the 4,000-mile journey home, where they arrived on a typical murky day. Air Marshal Sir Michael Stear, who had done so much to promote the Buccaneer's capability, flew to join the families for the very warm, emotional and well-deserved reception for a job well done. On return, Rick Phillips summed up his feelings shared by many others: 'I had often said that if I ever had to go to war, then the Buccaneer would be my first-choice aircraft. I was not wrong! I had total faith in our magnificent aeroplane.'

Homeward bound on the non-stop nine-hour direct flight, the Buccaneers met up with Victor tankers to refuel, with Mount Etna in the background. (*Dave Bolsover*)

CHAPTER 10

Last of the Buccaneers

On their return from the Gulf War, having performed in an outstanding manner, the Buccaneer force was at the height of its capabilities twenty-eight years after first entering squadron service with the Royal Navy. The embodiment of the new equipments under ASR 1012 and the new tactics based on the tremendous hitting power of Sea Eagle had made the Buccaneer the most powerful anti-shipping attack aircraft in NATO. The upgrade programme had been completed in 1989 and it was visualised that the force would remain in service until the end of the 1990s. However, the end of the Cold War had generated a number of defence reviews, resulting in some Tornado GR 1 aircraft being declared surplus to requirement. Plans were drawn up to equip two squadrons of these aircraft and modify them to carry Sea Eagle and replace the Buccaneers in the maritime role.

The steady run-down of the Buccaneer force started with the disbandment of 237 OCU on 1 October 1991, when its Buccaneers and Hunters were distributed to the two operational squadrons. A small Training Flight was established on 208 Squadron to convert the few remaining crews required to maintain the wing's capabilities. The last operational pilot trained on the Buccaneer was Flying Officer Ned Cullen, who neatly summed up the aircraft in one word,

This outstanding 208 Squadron Seventy-fifth Anniversary scheme did not meet with universal approval from higher authority and it had to be 'toned down'. Here it is seen shortly after roll-out from the paint shop at RAF Abingdon in October 1991. (*Flt Lt M Hudson, AHB Crown Copyright*)

Buccaneers of 237 OCU had a war role as Pave Spike 'markers' for Jaguars, Tornadoes and Dutch F 16s. These two aircraft carry the Pave Spike pod and display the familiar red hydraulic weeps streaming down the bomb bay. (*BAe Systems*)

'awesome'. On 1 January 1993 12 Squadron, after twenty-three years' continuous service, ceased to operate the Buccaneer: it became a Tornado squadron. The run-down of the Lossiemouth Buccaneer Wing did not, however, herald a relaxed time for 208 Squadron. In many respects the RAF's last Buccaneer squadron found itself in even greater demand as it fulfilled many exercise commitments and requests from the Royal Navy to assist in ships' operational work-up programmes.

Following the cessation of hostilities in the Gulf War, the Allied Coalition deployed naval forces in the area to monitor activities in the Persian Gulf, and the Royal Navy's 'Armilla Patrol' was established. The Buccaneers played a major part in the pre-deployment training exercises carried out by ships en route to the Gulf, and regular detachments were established at Gibraltar, often at squadron strength. Outside the UK, Gibraltar was host to more Buccaneer detachments than any other airfield, and local flying was always interesting. It was one of the few places where there was no requirement for Buccaneers to fly above 100 ft from take-off to landing. Squadrons had plenty of unrestricted

On 14 May 1992, Squadron Leader Dave Bolsover of 12 Squadron was flying XW 543 when it suffered a massive hydraulic failure and all services, including the undercarriage, airbrake and flaps, failed to operate. He and his navigator, Flight Lieutenant Steve Gregory, completed an immaculate belly landing at St Mawgan. The sequence shows the canopy being jettisoned, the aircraft touching down, the crew making a rapid exit, the aircraft settled on the runway and the recovery. Dave Bolsover was awarded a Green Endorsement for his 'exceptional flying skill'. (*MOD/Crown Copyright*)

sea-space to practise their Martel or, more latterly, Sea Eagle tactics, and there was also the added interest of finding a Soviet warship trying to transit the Straits unnoticed, and Buccaneers were often tasked to search for them. Squadron Leader John Fraser recalls the unique aspects of flying from Gibraltar's runway:

> Take-off and landing at Gibraltar in a Buccaneer was often a character building experience. The runway was 6,000 ft long and built out over the sea at both ends, with a busy road crossing it halfway down (the main access to Spain and called, rather unimaginatively, 'the Spanish Road'). For the majority of the time that Buccaneers operated from the airfield, emergency arresting was provided by a CHAG – CHain Arresting Gear. The CHAG was a very primitive piece of equipment consisting of a pile of chain on either side of the runway connected by a cable held clear of the ground by half-tyres. When engaged, it provided drag in a similar way to a ship being launched. The CHAG was positioned about 1,000 ft from the end of the runway, and provided over-run stopping assistance only. Furthermore, Buccaneer heavyweight take-off performance was such that the CHAG was often trampled, or had the supporting tyres blown over during the initial ground roll, so Air Traffic Control would provide a chap to sit in a Landrover at the side of the runway and reposition the tyres when necessary. Only individual take-offs were permitted, and this made a four or six-ship departure a very protracted affair. Despite the Buccaneer's famously unreliable hydraulic system, CHAG engagements were rare. However, I recall one occasion when an aircraft of our sister squadron engaged it during a high-speed abort, the only 'casualty' was the poor tyre-setter found sitting shocked in his Landrover after the event – not surprisingly, he'd never seen two tons of chain accelerate past his nose in a cloud of rust before, and the local laundry was grateful for his custom immediately afterwards.

The Buccaneer's slow-speed handling characteristics have been well documented, and local Gibraltar weather would often compound these problems. With the very large Rock of Gibraltar directly south and close to the runway, a wind with a southerly component created a crosswind from that sector and often produced dangerous turbulence, and up and down

draughts. Indeed, the wind speed limit for landing could be as low as 14 kts if the wind was from a critical direction. In addition, the 'Levant' wind caused a local phenomenon that regularly produced low cloud and poor visibility on the leeward side of the rock. To further compound problems, Spanish airspace started just 2 miles to the west of the airfield, so a curved final approach had to be made to the easterly runway, and if a radar approach was necessary the minima was relatively high due to the limitations of the procedure. These factors presented many unusual problems for aircrew, and even a slight shift of the wind could dramatically affect a take-off or landing technique. Dave Herriot recalls one incident from earlier days that illustrates the potential hazards of taking off:

> It had been a most marvellous weekend training flight to Gibraltar. It was midsummer, and I had been fortunate enough to be stranded in Gibraltar for five days with Norman Crow and a very sick XT274. We had flown down as a pair and our colleagues had returned to Honington after the weekend. We watched them depart as we sat drinking our brandy sours and soaking up the sun on the patio of North Front Officers' Mess on that beautiful August day. However, all good things had to end and XT274 came back to life late morning on the Wednesday. The temperature at 11.00 a.m. had reached plus 30°C. Norman and I had already decided that it was too late to attempt a take-off at that temperature from Gib's 6,000 ft of tarmac with water at both ends and only a rather ancient CHAG to arrest any forward momentum, should we realise too late that Algeciras Bay was approaching faster than V rotate! Unfortunately, whilst assessing how long we would have to wait until the Officers' Mess bar opened at lunchtime, we were called to the telephone to take 'a call from the CFI' at Honington. All our protestations about high outside air temperature and lack of Buccaneer performance in these conditions were to no avail, and we were ordered back home that very day! Norman and I consulted the Operating Data Manual (ODM) and began to construct our flight plan. The aircraft was equipped with two Martel training missiles on the outer pylons and a full complement of fuel giving it an all up weight of 52,000 lb. With BLC or 'blow' available, we could select different configurations for take-off or landing to suit the prevailing

Gibraltar provided superb facilities for training in the maritime role and hosted many Buccaneer detachments. This picture will bring back very many happy memories to those who enjoyed the flying and the hospitality of the people of Gibraltar. (*BAe Systems*)

conditions (either weather or airfield or both). We had two options; 15-10-10 unblown or 30-20-20 blown and the ODM was explicit. The Take Off Distance (TOD) required was either 6,100 ft unblown or 5,900 ft blown. With only 6,000 ft available there was only one choice – 30-20-20 blown it had to be. Norman spoke to the ATC local controller prior to getting into the cockpit and informed him that we would need every inch of the runway on take-off. He also informed him that we would require the latest temperature before brakes off and a guarantee that the overshoot was clear of any boats. We taxied out and almost reversed onto the orange and black chequers that mark the 'round down' on the easterly end of Gib's runway. When all was ready, Norman set the throttles in the top left hand corner and advised ATC that he was ready to roll, but would be grateful for the temperature and clearance before he released the brakes; 'plus thirty-two and clear' came the reply. 'What difference will two degrees hotter make, Dave?' he asked. 'Sorry, mate, don't know. ODM's in the bomb bay' I replied. 'Clear for take off' chimed ATC and we were rolling! Acceleration did not seem to happen although very imperceptibly the speed was increasing but, as we crossed the Spanish Road, I was having second thoughts about our decision not to go to the bar! However, as the Buccaneer got to the 100 ft 'distance to go' board (5,900 ft gone) the aircraft leapt into the air and steadied at about fifteen feet above the sea. At this moment Norman called out 'Oh Shit' which, under some circumstances, can sound like 'Eject!' but on this occasion it was quickly followed up with 'Look

Final departure from Gibraltar's westerly runway and Flight Lieutenant Mike Wood captures the moment as the number two closes up. (*Mike Wood*)

behind you' which ensured that I remained firmly connected to the aircraft. As Norman banked the lumbering Buccaneer onto a southerly track to avoid Spanish airspace I did as I was bid and, to my surprise, saw three Spanish fishermen swimming feverishly back towards their upturned rowing boat. Jet-wash at ultra-low level can have a most devastating effect on the unwary! The rest of the sortie back to Honington was uneventful and the CFI was very pleased to have his aircraft back. As for the Spanish fishermen; I can only guess they were poaching within Gibraltar waters, as we never heard another word on the subject!

The last Buccaneer detachment to Gibraltar occurred in February 1994 when 208 Squadron, under the command of Wing Commander Nigel Huckins, deployed for two weeks to provide air targets for the Royal Navy's Principal Weapons Officer (PWO) Course run on HMS *Liverpool*, a Type 42 destroyer. Daily flying consisted of two four-ship waves, each simulating Sea Eagle attacks, against the *Liverpool* whose trainee PWOs were tasked with coordinating and

During their last full year of service in the RAF, the Buccaneer Wing was honoured by being tasked to lead the Queen's Birthday Flypast on 12 June 1993. The aircraft are formed up in a 'Diamond Sixteen' approaching London. (*BAe Systems*)

controlling the ship's defences to thwart the threat. This was a particularly difficult task, since a real attack would have culminated in two high-speed salvos of up to twelve missiles each arriving from different directions at 10–15 ft above sea level.

The final Buccaneer detachment attracted a lot of interest from the local population and media, indicating the significance of the event and the warm regard with which those who had enjoyed its regular presence over the years held the aircraft. The detachment was a complete success, and so it was an emotional experience for all concerned when the aircraft left the Rock for the final time.

To acknowledge its outstanding RAF service over many years, the Buccaneer was chosen to lead the Queen's Birthday Flypast in 1993, just a few months before it was withdrawn from service. Leading the formation in this unique occasion was Squadron Leader Rick Phillips and his navigator, Wing Commander Nigel Maddox. The formation chosen for the Buccaneers was a demanding sixteen-ship diamond made up of four sections of four aircraft with a reserve section acting as a spare. Rick Phillips explains the sortie:

> It had been decided to mount the Buccaneer formation from Manston to cut transit times to a minimum for the practices. One essential event for

me as the leader was a helicopter trip down the route a week before the flypast. This was invaluable, and to this day I can still visualise the salient features, which were glued into the brain as markers. Thereafter, all the practices went well. From previous experience, I wanted to be sure of the weather on the day [12 June 1993] – I had been the victim of other people's decisions on these big flypasts before. Consequently, when I briefed, I had only just left the route, and had a firm feel for the situation. We checked in on the radio, with our call-sign for the day 'Blackburn', and taxied out on time. With all aircraft fully serviceable, it was a wonderful sight to see twenty Buccaneers, and the whip Hunter, follow me from the ramp at Manston with wings folded. A huge crowd of well-wishers waved us off as we taxied to the runway, and we gave them a final flypast in diamond sixteen. Thereafter, it was on track and on time the whole way, with Nigel Maddox doing an outstanding job, whilst I concentrated on smooth flying and, most importantly, good lookout for puddle-jumpers. Sure enough, one pitched up right on the nose some 20 miles before the Palace, with a cameraman filming us out of the side door as we flew straight at him – just what you don't need with an unwieldy formation. We over-flew the Palace on time, and turned away to recover to Lossiemouth for a final sixteen-ship diamond flypast. Only then did I realise what an enormous strain I had been under; to have made any errors at all on such a sortie was unthinkable. I was relieved that it had all gone so well, which of course was the result of good training, excellent aircrew and, not least, a fantastic aeroplane.

After landing, the aircrew were met by the media. One journalist asked Rick Phillips what it was like to fly the Buccaneer. His reply, 'just like flying a ball-bearing on glass', neatly sums up every Buccaneer aircrew's feelings.

It was not in the nature of the Buccaneer men to go quietly, and a weekend of major events was

The aircrew pose in front of their aircraft at Manston before taking off for the Anniversary flypast. Leader of the formation was Squadron Leader Rick Phillips with his navigator Wing Commander Nigel Maddox. They are seated at the front. The two Hunters were used as 'whippers in' to ensure that the formation was correctly spaced. (*Norman Browne*)

For the final farewell in March 1994 seven aircraft received the markings of the squadrons that had flown the Buccaneer. XX 894 was painted in the markings of 809 Squadron to represent all the Royal Navy Buccaneer squadrons and was flown by the Squadron Commander of 208 Squadron, Wing Commander Nigel Huckins. The aircraft are stepped up in numerical order of squadrons, 12, XV, 16, 208, 216 and 237 OCU. (*MOD Crown Copyright*)

organised at Lossiemouth to say farewell to the faithful old aircraft. As the last Buccaneer unit, it fell to 208 Squadron to send the aircraft into retirement in style. The Squadron Commander, Nigel Huckins, had already hit on the brilliant idea of repainting the aircraft to represent every RAF Buccaneer squadron, but his most inspiring idea was to paint XX 894 in the full Royal Navy colours of 809 Squadron – and this gesture was received with acclaim. It epitomised the strength of the Buccaneer fraternity. Furthermore, he chose to fly the aircraft and lead all the farewell formations.

Over the weekend of 26–27 March 1994, 1,100 former Royal Navy and RAF Buccaneer air and ground crews and their families made the pilgrimage to join 208 Squadron at a spectacular finale. The scale of the event was huge, with people arriving by road, rail and air – a wide variety of aircraft flew into Lossiemouth. There were many VIP visitors, and Buccaneer men arrived from Australia, USA, South Africa and Hong Kong. The scale of support served to remind people of the huge affection for the aircraft that existed, and it was fitting that

Lossiemouth was the venue since it was at RNAS Lossiemouth, HMS *Fulmar*, that the Buccaneer first entered service.

The highlight of the weekend occurred at 2.00 p.m. on the Saturday, when Nigel Huckins, in XX 894, taxied out at the head of nine Buccaneers. They lined up on Lossiemouth's runway 23 for a ten-second-stream take-off, with each pilot appearing to retract the undercarriage almost before the aircraft became airborne. A few moments later the team returned in an immaculate 'Diamond Nine' formation. Flight Lieutenants Glen Mason and Gary Davies broke from the formation to give their final solo display, before the nine Buccaneers did what the aircraft did best. They appeared at very, very low level and 580 kts on a 'simulated airfield attack' from different directions in an ear-shattering roar. After landing, they taxied passed the waiting crowds and returned to the flight line, where, on a command from Nigel Huckins, all nine aircraft folded their wings in unison in a symbolic gesture of farewell. Even the most hard-nosed of Buccaneer men had a lump in his throat, and there was hardly a dry eye on the airfield.

The afternoon event was brought to a close by a series of short farewell speeches led by Vice-Admiral Sir 'Ted' Anson, who had done so much to bring the Buccaneer into Royal Navy service. He was followed by Air Chief Marshal Sir Michael Knight, a former Buccaneer Station

The withdrawal of the Buccaneer was also the finale in RAF service for the Hunter, which had given such wonderful service as a fighter and later as a training aircraft in the Buccaneer force, for over thirty years. Seen here is WV 318 that has been preserved and can still be seen in the skies over Kemble. (*Dave Bolsover*)

After the superb farewell flypast at Lossiemouth on 27 March 1995, XW 527 representing 16 Squadron taxies back for the last time to a very nostalgic reception. (*MOD Crown Copyright*)

Commander at Laarbruch and Air Officer Commanding No. 1 Group when he had four Buccaneer squadrons under command. Finally, Dr Mike Edwards, who had been so involved in the development of the aircraft as an engineer and flight test observer at Blackburns and later British Aerospace, spoke of the unique relationship that had always existed between the Buccaneer force and the workforce at Brough, the home of the aircraft. The presence of these three distinguished men, representing the key elements of the Buccaneer era, was more than symbolic. It reinforced the message that the Buccaneer and its air and ground crews was, indeed, a unique force built around a great aircraft – 'The Last all-British Bomber'. As the old song goes:

Give me Buccaneers,
They're British through and through
The banana jet, the best we've had yet,
We are the last of the few.

Farewell! (*BAe Systems*)

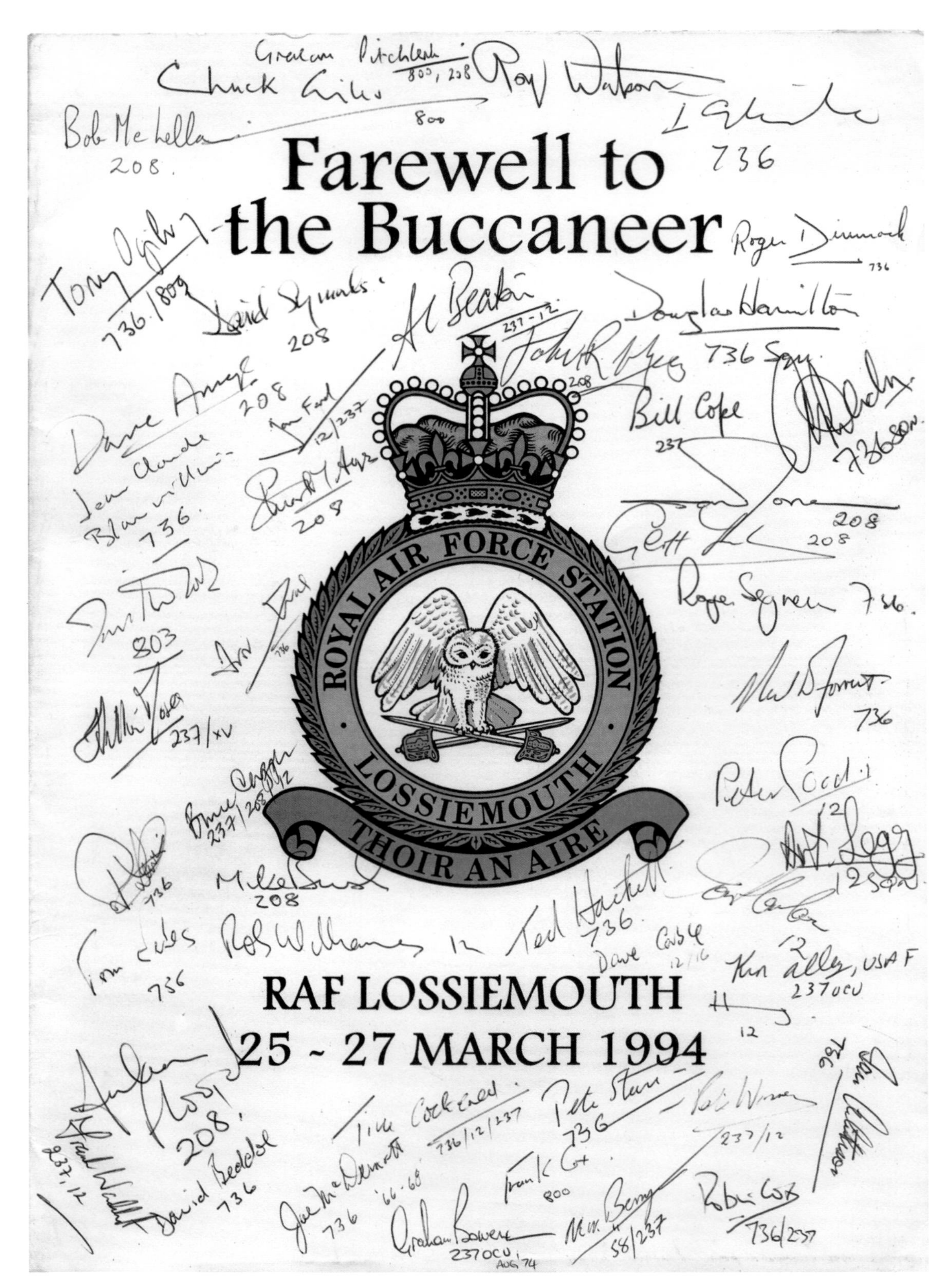

Buccaneer pilots sign the Farewell programme.

Epilogue

On 31 March 1994, 208 Squadron ceased to be declared to NATO, and the Buccaneer's thirty-two years of operational service were over. It also signalled the end of the Hunter in RAF service, and both types started to leave Lossiemouth, many to be scrapped and others to be used as training aids. Some found their way to museums to be displayed for future generations to admire. Indeed, one XX 901, was actually purchased by members of the recently formed Buccaneer Aircrew Association (BAA) to rest proudly in 'Gulf War pink' livery, and surrounded by an impressive display of Buccaneer weaponry and associated operational components at the Yorkshire Air Museum's fine Elvington site. However, the sad fact remains that after mid-April 1994 no RAF Buccaneer flew again. Three aircraft operated by the Defence Research Agency (formerly the RAE) continued to fly until February of the following year. Two of these, XW 987 and XW 988, were bought by a South African collector and ferried to Cape Town, where they continue to thrill the air show crowds.

The first and only Buccaneer landing on the very short 3,450-ft runway at Brough was made on 15 October 1993 when Squadron Leader Rick Phillips and Wing Commander Nigel Maddox delivered XV 168 for static display at the British Aerospace factory, where all Buccaneers started life. (*Author's collection*)

Personnel at the Brough British Aerospace factory had to evacuate the office block at the end of the short runway. It was completely unnecessary as they all turned out to see the arrival of XV 168. Throughout the life of the Buccaneer, there had always been a very close relationship and respect between those who built the aircraft and those who flew and serviced it. (*BAe Systems*)

MOD (PE) operated the last three British military Buccaneers. The aircraft were used extensively for weapons trials, and all three are now flying in South Africa. XW 987, with wing-tip-mounted cameras to monitor weapon release from the wing stations, flying low near West Freugh. (*MOD/Crown copyright*)

One of the ex-MOD (PE) aircraft – the former XW 988 – flying near Cape Town, where the aircraft is kept in immaculate flying order by Mike Beachyhead at Thunder City. (*Duncan Cubitt/Flypast*)

The Buccaneer Aircrew Association met at the Yorkshire Air Museum for the roll-out of their Gulf War veteran aircraft XX 901 on 11 October 1996. It is on permanent display, together with a wide range of weapons carried by the aircraft. (*Author*)

APPENDIX

In Memoriam

Name	Unit	Date	Aircraft
Mr W.H. Aldred	A&AEE	12.10.59	XK 490
Mr J. Joyce	Blackburns	12.10.59	XK 490
Lt Cdr O. Brown	A&AEE	31.8.61	XK 529
Mr T. Dunn	Blackburns	31.8.61	XK 529
Lt G.W.N. Jones	A&AEE	5.7.62	XN 922
Lt W.W. Foote USN	700Z Flt	18.8.62	XK 535
Lt M.J. Day	700Z Flt	18.8.62	XK 535
Mr G.R.I. Parker	Hawker Siddeley	19.2.63	XN 952
Mr G.R.C. Copeman	Hawker Siddeley	19.2.63	XN 952
Lt Cdr P.H. Perks	801 Sqn	26.11.64	XN 948
Lt Cdr W.H.C. Watson	736 Sqn	25.6.65	XN 961
Lt A.J. Hume	736 Sqn	25.6.65	XN 961
Sub Lt C.D.C. Councell	736 Sqn	28.3.66	XN 950
Flt Lt W.K. Mackinson	A &AEE	30.6.66	XK 528
Flt Lt C.M. Pridmore	A &AEE	30.6.66	XK 528
Plt Off P.J. Paines	736 Sqn	8.12 70	XN 968
Wg Cdr D.J.H. Collins	XV Sqn	25.3.71	XW 532
Flt Lt P. Kelly	XV Sqn	25.3.71	XW 532
Sqn Ldr T.G. Gilroy	Honington Wing	4.1.72	XW 539
Flt Lt C. Willbourne	12 Sqn	4.1.72	XW 539
Capt G. Vipond USAF	12 Sqn	13.6.72	XV 162
Flt Lt D. Walmsley	12 Sqn	13.6.72	XV 162
Flt Lt D. Mann	809 Sqn	12.4.73	XV 343
Lt S. Kershaw	809 Sqn	11.11.74	XV 351
Lt D.H.J. Owen	237 OCU	31.10.77	XV 348
Mr Love	British Aerospace	5.7.78	XT 285
Mr J.R. Bigland	British Aerospace	5.7.78	XT 285
Flt Lt A. Colvin	16 Sqn	12.7.79	XW 526
Sqn Ldr D. Coupland	16 Sqn	12.7.79	XW 526
Sqn Ldr K.J. Tait	XV Sqn	7.2.80	XV 345
Flt Lt C.R. Ruston	XV Sqn	7.2.80	XV 345
Flt Lt S. Dakin	16 Sqn	11.8.83	XX 891
Sqn Ldr W. Graham	208 Sqn	20.5.84	XZ 430
Flt Lt A. White	208 Sqn	20.5.84	XZ 430
Flt Lt W. Steele	12 Sqn	14.6.85	XV 341
Flt Lt J.J. Cooke	12 Sqn	22.4.87	XW 540
Fg Off A. Fahy	12 Sqn	22.4.87	XW 540
Flt Lt J. Henderson	208 Sqn	9.7.92	XN 976
Flt Lt C. Lambourne	208 Sqn	9.7.92	XN 976

Index

Figures in *italics* refer to illustrations